Donald R. Levi, DREI

How To Teach Adults

A Handbook for Real Estate Instructors

Second Edition

 Real Estate Educators Association

Copyright © 1989, 1996 by the Real Estate Educators Association. All rights reserved including the right of reproduction in whole or in part in any form. Published by the Real Estate Educators Association, 11 South LaSalle Street, Suite 1400, Chicago, Illinois, 60603-1210

ISBN 0-9621154-1-X

CONTENTS

Preface	i
1. Overview of Instructor Development	1
2. Adult Learning	17
3. The Learning Environment	33
4. Teaching Methods	47
5. Dealing with Common Classroom Situations	59
6. Preparing and Presenting Classroom Materials	73
7. Effective Use of Humor	93
8. Dress and Body Language	101
9. Audio-Visual Aids	109
10. The Master Classroom	127
11. Teaching to Remote Locations	141
12. Preparing Exams and Examination Questions	153
Appendix A: Generally Accepted Principles of Education	177
Appendix B: Promoting Adult Education Courses	181
Index	191

Preface

This second edition includes a number of significant changes. First and foremost, the research literature now suggests that children and adults are not necessarily different in ways that affect how learning occurs. However, from the standpoint of instructors, the techniques that formerly were thought to work best for adults now are recognized to work equally well when teaching children. This implies that the andragogical concepts set out in REEA's Generally Accepted Principles of Education are still valid.

A second significant addition is that of learning styles. Understanding that different students have differing learning styles is basic to meeting the needs of all students. Although students seldom learn by a single style, teaching to meet the needs of visual, audio (aural), tactual and kinesthetic learners is a goal toward which we should all strive.

This edition also contains new chapters about teaching in technologically modern classrooms and beaming educational presentations to remote locations. Today's challenge is to utilize modern technology as a teaching tool while retaining presentation techniques which communicate well. It will be interesting to see how much future teaching is done via the Internet, and whether/how the Internet changes the ways in which we teach.

The material has been updated throughout as we have learned more about effective classroom communication. As an example, since brains can only process so much material at one time, under appropriate circumstances "chunking" together concepts and material may cause students to learn more. Statistical methods for evaluating how well examination questions discriminate among knowledge levels is another addition important to those charged with the responsibility of grading learning performance.

A number of people deserve recognition for reviewing and making suggested changes in this edition, including Karen Post, DREI, and Cindy Clark from REEA headquarters staff. I want to particularly acknowledge the substantive suggestions of Marie Spodek, DREI, and Julie Garton-Good, DREI. Although not directly involved in the review process, several authors of *REEAction* articles who were cited via chapter end notes also indirectly contributed to the content of this edition. I thank them for sharing their ideas and expanding the teaching knowledge base. I also thank the hundreds of REEA Instructor Development Workshop participants who shared what works well for them, and which contributed to my thinking on many topics covered in this edition. Pete Polak, MBA student and graduate assistant, deserves special thanks for handling the myriad of computer-based challenges required to provide camera-ready copy to the printer.

Because this edition still borrows much from the first, I wish to thank those who made meaningful contributions to the initial effort. In no particular order, they include: John W. Reilly, DREI, Charles J. Jacobus, DREI, Dr. Mark Dotzour and Norma Gribble of Wichita State University; and Jeri Pyeatt, Director of the Idaho Real Estate Commission.

Dr. Donald R. Levi, DREI
Wichita State University
March, 1996

CHAPTER ONE

Overview of Instructor Development

Introduction

In recent years, total quality management (TQM) has dominated management thought in the business world. Many management gurus admit that TQM contains few (if any) new concepts, but rather represents a repackaging of old truths. The principal buzzword phrase of TQM is "continuous improvement," and the TQM goal of "continuous improvement" is equally applicable to business management and real estate teaching.

From a TQM perspective, the purpose of this book is to help real estate educators continuously improve. It is designed to help beginning instructors to more quickly become proficient in teaching adults, and to provide veteran educators new ideas and techniques that will improve their classroom performances. In short, the goal of this book is to assist real estate instructors in their continuing quest for professional improvement.

Teaching adults is both challenging and rewarding, yet sometimes frustrating. Instructors teaching adults need to have (1) knowledge of the subject matter they teach, (2) the ability to communicate effectively, and (3) an appreciation of the unique problems and goals of adult learners. To quote a fellow REEA member[1] "Teaching is like most things - ninety percent of success is due to preparation." The most successful real estate teachers not only have the ability to convert basic principles and theory into real life situations, but are thoroughly prepared to do so using a variety of teaching methods. This book is designed to assist in developing and improving these abilities, and to outline a number of important ideas for consideration when preparing to teach.

An Overview of This Book

Many readers have attended classes that were nearly over before they figured out what the instructors were trying to accomplish and "where the instructors were going" with their presentations. Students appreciate instructors who take a few moments at the beginning of class to outline both what will be covered and the practical importance of the material to be presented. This helps adult students determine how a class will help them meet their personal and professional goals.

In the same manner, people reading textbooks like to know the content and order of the material to be presented. Thus, the reader may want to briefly review the table of contents in this book. Although some will read first the chapters of greatest interest, reading the chapters in order may be a more efficient learning experience because the material presented in an early chapter may increase readers' understanding of materials discussed later.

Chapter One begins with a brief overview of what instructor development is all about. It emphasizes such items as the importance of becoming familiar with the background of students, how teaching efficiency can be improved through feedback from students, and how student background information and feedback may be obtained.

The **second chapter** raises the basic questions of whether or not adults and children are different in ways other than physical development and maturity. If such differences exist, then it is possible that adults may learn differently than children. If this is true, then the choice and efficiency of teaching techniques and supporting learning materials may be affected.

Chapter Three surveys methods of stimulating adult learning, including the basic resources from which adults may learn. The four basic resources impacting on the quality of the learning process include the physical environment, instructors, written materials, and other students in the class.

Chapter Four outlines various teaching methods. Several factors affect the choice of teaching methods, including student backgrounds, the topic to be taught, and the skills, preferences, and personal style of instructors. If adults are different from children in ways that impact on learning, then it is logical to conclude that the time-tested methods used to teach children may not be equally efficient in teaching adults.

Suggestions for handling some common problem situations that arise in the classroom are covered in **Chapter Five**. These classroom scenarios include students who attempt to dominate a class, as well as others. Since the manner in which these problems are handled significantly affects the efficiency of the learning process, as well as the rapport existing between the instructor and his/her students, specific solutions are provided.

Chapter Six covers the preparation and presentation of materials. It includes such important topics as alternative methods for organizing materials, techniques for immediately attracting and retaining the attention of students, and helping students gain the confidence that they can successfully implement the principles being taught.

Bored students often are not receptive to learning, so **Chapter Seven** discusses the use of humor in the classroom. When properly employed, humor can be of great assistance in emphasizing and helping students remember important points. At the same time, humor is not a substitute for the presentation of substantive materials. Furthermore, inappropriate humor sometimes detracts from the learning process.

Chapter Eight discusses appropriate instructor dress and body language. Attention to both can enhance the learning environment.

Chapter Nine outlines the audio-visual aids available to today's instructors, discussing the strengths and weaknesses of each. Classroom size and layout, the type and magnitude of written materials distributed, the topics being taught, and instructors' personal styles combine to influence the choice of audio-visual aids.

Chapters Ten and Eleven are both new to the second edition. Chapter Ten discusses the advantages and challenges presented in "master classrooms" which offer the latest in audio-visual aids technology. The eleventh chapter looks at some concerns facing instructors teaching to remote locations via various broadcast media.

The **twelfth chapter** is of particular interest to those charged with the responsibility of grading and/or preparing students for examinations. It discusses how different types of questions may be prepared and utilized for testing, and how the performance of individual test items may be analyzed. It also points out that examinations potentially may be both a teaching device as well as a method of evaluating student learning.

The **Appendix** contains two items of interest. First, it contains the Generally Accepted Principles of Education (GAPE) which have been adopted by REEA[2]. Second, the appendix also briefly discusses various promotional methods by which instructors and schools may attract students. These promotional methods include posters, flyers, direct mail, and newspaper, radio, and television advertising. Promotion/teaching via the Internet is also briefly explored.

Professionalism in Real Estate Teaching

Professionalism has been a byword in the real estate industry for many years. Real estate brokerage mandatory prelicense, postlicense, and continuing education requirements have increased the level of professionalism and resulted in additional protection to the public served by real estate licensees. Growth in real estate educational course offerings has been derived from both mandatory educational requirements and the desire of individual licensees for additional education. This desire for increased professionalism in the real estate brokerage industry has led to the development of a voluntary association that teachers and others with an interest in the quality of real estate education can join and learn by sharing ideas. In point of fact, a major goal of the Real Estate Educators Association (REEA) is increasing professionalism among real estate educators. Another major goal of REEA is to improve the quality of real estate education.

Thorough knowledge of the subject matter to be taught must be possessed by professional educators. Those who do not possess this knowledge will receive low ratings from students, even with the use of superb supporting written materials and audio-visual aids. Likewise, providing students with top-notch study materials may not completely overcome a dull monotone lecture. Rather, knowledge, sound supporting study materials, organization, and strong communication skills are the hallmark of professional educators.

Professional educators also have social responsibilities. To illustrate, students may be more likely to engage in ethical conduct if their instructors emphasize ethical responsibilities to the general public.

In an effort to communicate what professionalism means to real estate teachers, the 1990 REEA Board of Directors adopted a document entitled "Generally Accepted Principles of Education." Popularly referred to as "GAPE," this document makes specific suggestions for instructors in five different categories: Knowledge, andragogy (defined in Chapter Two), speech, teaching aids, and the learning environment. GAPE is reproduced in the appendix, and the reader will find it useful to review this document before reading further. The suggestions set out in GAPE are helpful to teachers at all levels of instruction.

Professional real estate educators are evaluated on the basis of how they look, what they do, what they say, and how they say it. This book is intended to assist instructors in becoming more professional by discussing these and other important topics.

The Importance of Getting Acquainted With the Class

Homogeneous classes composed of students with similar backgrounds, needs, and goals are easier to teach than those containing students with different backgrounds, needs, and goals. Adult real estate students may range in age from 18 to 80+, with an average age of around 40. Educational backgrounds may vary from high school diploma equivalencies (GEDs) to Ph.D.s. Students in prelicense courses often come from a broad variety of occupational backgrounds. Post-license and continuing education students working in real estate brokerage may have vastly different jobs, needs, and goals depending in part on the specific segment of the real estate industry in which they specialize. This difference in student background is further emphasized by the fact that post-license/continuing education courses also often include a number of attendees whose major employment is in some phase of the real estate industry other than brokerage. In any event, teaching can occur more efficiently if instructors are knowledgeable about students' backgrounds, needs, and goals when class begins. Instructors may obtain this knowledge in a number of ways.

Reviewing forms filled out by students when preregistering for class is a simple way to obtain some basic background information. Some preregistration forms may need to be redesigned in order to obtain this information. By way of example, if the impact of federal income taxes on real estate is the topic to be taught, the preregistration blank might contain boxes that can be checked indicating whether each preregistrant real estate licensee primarily sells single-family residential or commercial properties. Summarizing these responses will help instructors determine if time could be better spent discussing income tax rules affecting the sale of family residences or like-kind exchanges.

Information about student backgrounds can also be obtained at the beginning of class. For example, instructors might ask individual students to introduce themselves, stating their names, hometowns, employing firms, and nature of their jobs. A short explanation of future plans and goals might also be requested. In larger classes, the same information may be acquired by asking for a show of hands in response to a few important background questions.

Some will argue that taking time for student introductions is not feasible. Certainly this is true if there are 1,000 students in the classroom. On the other hand, in small classes the time used for student introductions and obtaining background information may be more than offset by increased learning efficiency when instructors are able to tailor their presentations according to the background of the class.

Taking a few moments "up front" to obtain background information about students also serves to "break the ice". Students tend to be more confident of their ability to succeed in class, as well as less tense and less afraid of the unknown, when they realize that others in the class come from similar backgrounds. Dividing the class into non-acquainted pairs, permitting each person to elicit information about his or her partner, and then allowing each a minute or so to introduce the other is an excellent way to break the ice. In fact, many instructors find this technique a more effective ice breaker than student self-introductions.

Occasionally, instructors ask students to introduce themselves at either the middle or end of the program. This may help students identify their classmates for later professional contact, but does little to help instructors determine which topics in their presentation should receive special emphasis.

Another good way to break the ice and also obtain information about students' backgrounds and educational needs is to give a short pretest covering the topics to be taught. In this way, instructors can quickly gain information influencing the amount of time to be devoted to each topic.

In addition to being familiar with student backgrounds, instructors also need to be aware of why students are attending their classes. When students' reasons for attending are dissimilar to instructors' perceived purposes for the class, less than optimal learning may occur.

Stated somewhat differently, educational needs continually change. To illustrate, since real estate markets tend to be cyclical, skills needed by real estate professionals also change with movement through the business cycle. Real estate courses must be designed not only to meet these changing educational needs, but also to meet the needs of all students (e.g., new salespeople and experienced sales people; and new home, existing home, commercial investment, farm and ranch, and property management specialists). Classes must also accommodate changing needs resulting from non-cyclical factors such as changing laws and income tax rules, construction technology, and the like. The important point is that the most successful courses are those designed to fulfill relevant and identified needs, and this involves being knowledgeable about why students are attending.

Differences in age, educational levels, and needs are not the only background characteristics of which instructors need to be aware. Those working in real estate brokerage tend to be market-oriented, quite competitive, and perhaps even demanding. Instructors need to be aware of characteristics such as these when selecting teaching techniques that communicate with maximum effectiveness. Stated differently, instructors must be aware of students' personal and psychological, as well as intellectual, needs.

Finally, class discussion and involvement will be encouraged when instructors call on students by name. For this reason, name tags with large letters and tent cards placed on tables in front of each student are helpful aids to effective communication.

Choices of Level of Presentation

Few classes contain students with uniformly identical backgrounds, goals, and intellectual capabilities. Because of this fact, a common problem facing teachers is whether they should prepare their presentation to meet the needs of the lower, middle, or upper part of their class. The decision on instructional level may depend on the type of class being taught, as well as student expectations.

Frequently teachers tailor their presentation level to the middle of the class. Teaching for the upper level may stretch many students to the upper extent of their abilities with students from the lower level becoming completely lost. On the other hand, designing the presentation to primarily meet the needs of the lower end of the class typically results in students at higher levels learning little and being bored.

Often the variation in student levels is mainly due to weak backgrounds rather than in differences in the capacity to learn. If so, instructors may be able to accomplish the greatest amount of learning by starting at a basic level but moving quickly to a more advanced stage while providing a clear, logical explanation of basic and intermediate level materials.

Obtaining and Using Feedback

In the business world, feedback can mean the difference between Caribbean cruises and bankruptcy. Men and women in business need to know how they are doing and how they can improve their product or services. Feedback is equally essential for success in teaching. The best way to get feedback is to ask for it. Feedback which helps instructors improve can be obtained from both students and other instructors.

The most useful feedback is both specific and direct. That is, feedback should tell instructors what they are doing wrong (or right!) and the consequences of using various classroom teaching techniques. This type of feedback helps teachers improve.

But if feedback is too direct, it can hurt. Feedback (constructive criticism) from fellow instructors is more likely to be useful and received well when preceded by a compliment. Furthermore, it generally is not helpful when someone provides

349 items of "constructive criticism" at the same time. Simultaneously providing 349 suggestions for improvement may overwhelm new instructors, for example, and lead them to believe that they can never become superior teachers. Keep this idea in mind when offering constructive criticism to teaching colleagues.

When instructors ask students for feedback, they should be direct and specific. When teaching a particular concept, teachers might ask, "Does this concept make sense?" Sometimes they get a surprise answer. If so, instructors should ask if others agree. Also, if instructors are not sure what students mean when asking questions or making statements, they should ask the students to repeat the question or comment in a different way. Continually seeking feedback throughout class can help instructors reach and remain on the same "wave length" as their students. In this way, effective feedback improves the efficiency of the learning process. Good feedback should be verbally rewarded (praised) in order to encourage even more feedback as a class progresses.

Obviously, student feedback can be obtained either during or at the end of class. For that matter, feedback can also be obtained well after a class has been completed. However, only feedback obtained *during* class permits adjustments to be made in presentations so that more learning can occur in the present class.

Unfortunately, some instructors only obtain student feedback at the end of class if at all. At this stage, the current class is similar to water over the dam. Thus, the major benefit of end-of-class feedback is facilitating improvement for future classes.

Significant design differences exist among end-of-class evaluation sheets used by different schools and instructors. Although very useful to instructors, many students will not take the time at the end of class to write down what they liked most and least about the class. Picking up children from the babysitter, attending a PTA meeting or an appointment with a business prospect all tend to be more important to students leaving class than giving written feedback to instructors. And those students who ask to take the evaluation form home so it can be thoughtfully completed and mailed back later do not send the evaluation back in the majority of cases. Thus, as a practical matter, the space reserved for written comments on end-of-class evaluation sheets seldom provides as much information as desired.

However, the same feedback that could have been gleaned from written student comments may be obtained objectively if the evaluation sheet is structured properly. To do so, it should first be recognized that students do not spend much time filling out evaluation sheets, so making student responses as easy as possible will improve the response rate.

For example, the evaluation sheet may be structured in a similar manner to a research survey or questionnaire. The students can be asked to provide their evaluation on a scale of one (lowest) to ten (highest). They can be asked to simply circle the number which represents their evaluation of a number of specific aspects about the class. Space can also be provided for specific comments and constructive criticisms.

A formal course evaluation should cover students' appraisals of at least five specific areas: (1) quality of instruction; (2) usefulness/quality of handout materials; (3) substantive course content; (4) adequacy of the facilities; and (5) administrative functions (e.g., registration procedures). A brief example of an evaluation form which covers these areas and permits numerical responses is shown in figure 1-1.

Feedback also can be obtained several days, weeks, or even months after a class is over. Although many former students will not take the time to fill out and return post-class questionnaires, those who do return them have had the opportunity to reflect on the usefulness and relevance of the materials presented. In some instances, post-class evaluation summaries may differ significantly from end-of-class assessments. Thus, even though it is expensive, at least occasionally mailing out post-class evaluation forms may provide important feedback to instructors and course providers. It is important to recognize that teaching is not completed until all course and student evaluations are summarized.

Summary

This chapter provides an overview of instructor development/continuous improvement for professional real estate educators teaching adults. At the outset, two basic suggestions are offered. First, getting acquainted with students helps "break the ice" and develops a friendly rapport between students and instructors. Moreover, instructors familiar with students' backgrounds can tailor their presentations to meet the needs of each class, so it is imperative to learn about student backgrounds.

Second, instructors can improve their presentations and teaching abilities by continuously obtaining feedback from students. Feedback obtained during class helps instructors to ascertain how well they are communicating and to make needed changes in planned presentations to meet the needs of a particular class. Feedback obtained from formal class evaluations at the end of class or later aids in improving teaching techniques and materials for future classes.

Figure 1-1: Example of an Evaluation Form
HOW TO AVOID LAWSUITS SEMINAR EVALUATION
Chicago, Illinois - December 1, 1995

Please circle the number which represents your evaluation of each aspect of this seminar, using a scale of 1 (lowest) to 10 (highest). Your specific comments and suggestions are also solicited to further assist us in improving future seminars. Please use the back of the evaluation form if more space is required for your comments and suggestions.

I. Quality of Instruction. Please rate each of the seminar instructors:
1. Jane Doe   1 2 3 4 5 6 7 8 9 10
2. Richard Roe   1 2 3 4 5 6 7 8 9 10

Comments/suggestions on quality of instruction: _____

II. Written Handout Materials. Please rate each of the following:
1. Organization   1 2 3 4 5 6 7 8 9 10
2. Substantive content   1 2 3 4 5 6 7 8 9 10

Comments/suggestions on handout materials: _____

III. Course Content. Please evaluate each of the following topics:
1. Agency law (liability to sellers and buyers)   1 2 3 4 5 6 7 8 9 10
   A. Duty of obedience   1 2 3 4 5 6 7 8 9 10
   B. Duty of loyalty   1 2 3 4 5 6 7 8 9 10
   C. Duty of due care   1 2 3 4 5 6 7 8 9 10
   D. Duty of accounting   1 2 3 4 5 6 7 8 9 10
2. Misrepresentation law (liability to buyers)   1 2 3 4 5 6 7 8 9 10
   A. Fraudulent conduct   1 2 3 4 5 6 7 8 9 10
   B. Negligent conduct   1 2 3 4 5 6 7 8 9 10
3. Illustrative case studies   1 2 3 4 5 6 7 8 9 10
4. Methods to reduce risk of liability   1 2 3 4 5 6 7 8 9 10

Comments/suggestions on course content: _____

IV. Facilities. Please rate each of the following:
1. Location   1 2 3 4 5 6 7 8 9 10
2. Room size   1 2 3 4 5 6 7 8 9 10
3. Room arrangement   1 2 3 4 5 6 7 8 9 10
4. Room temperature   1 2 3 4 5 6 7 8 9 10
5. Refreshments at breaks   1 2 3 4 5 6 7 8 9 10
6. Meals   1 2 3 4 5 6 7 8 9 10
7. Seating comfort   1 2 3 4 5 6 7 8 9 10
8. Lighting   1 2 3 4 5 6 7 8 9 10
9. Parking   1 2 3 4 5 6 7 8 9 10
10. Telephone availability   1 2 3 4 5 6 7 8 9 10
11. Acoustics   1 2 3 4 5 6 7 8 9 10
12. Audio-visual equipment   1 2 3 4 5 6 7 8 9 10

Comments/suggestions on facilities: _____

V. Administrative Functions. Please rate each of the following:
1. Pre-registration procedures   1 2 3 4 5 6 7 8 9 10
2. Registration/check-in procedures at door   1 2 3 4 5 6 7 8 9 10
3. Procedure for distributing attendance certificates   1 2 3 4 5 6 7 8 9 10

Comments/suggestions on administrative functions: _____

VI. Recommendations. Would you recommend this class to:
1. a new licensee   ____ Yes   ____ No
2. an experienced licensee   ____ Yes   ____ No
3. What did you like best about the seminar? _____

4. What did you like least about the seminar? _____

Exercises for Chapter One

1. Suppose you are teaching a class on agency. What information should you seek from participants in order to tailor your workshop to their needs? Why is each bit of requested information important to you?

2. Prepare a list of simple questions which will help instructors obtain feedback from students during class.

3. Prepare a class evaluation form that will permit instructors to obtain desired feedback after a class has been completed.

End Notes

[1] Baze, Dale, "Benchmarking Quality in Real Estate Education," *REEAction*, January-February 1995, p. 7.
[2] 1993-94 REEA President Mark Barker, DREI, was the primary author of GAPE

CHAPTER TWO

Adult Learning

Introduction

For many years, a branch of educational theory suggested that adults learn differently than children. Malcolm Knowles was the acknowledged leader of this branch of adult learning, and those adopting his views argued that, logically, teaching techniques that are most efficient for adults may differ from those that work best when teaching children. Andragogy is the term used to describe the process by which adults learn. In contrast, the term pedagogy refers to the process by which children learn. In this chapter, we discuss perceived learning-related differences between adults and children and review research bearing on the question of whether or not adults really do learn differently than children. We begin with an analysis of pedagogy and andragogy. Pedagogy is the more familiar term, so it is discussed first.

Pedagogy

In the simplest sense, pedagogy is the process by which children learn those things they need to know in order to become functioning, productive members of our society. Some obvious examples include basic mathematics and English grammar. Most (but not all) pedagogical teaching processes involve situations where school (class) attendance is mandatory.

Children do not have broad lifetime experiences on which to draw, so a significant portion of their learning occurs by rote memorization. Many questions posed to children involve a single "right" answer. Teachers, together with groups within the organized educational system, determine the information which children need to learn. Along with the motivation to be successful in life, teachers also provide the inspiration for learning. Motivating children is made more difficult by the fact that the material being presented often is a part of a building block process which will be useful in the future rather than immediately. Also, the fact that learned materials will not be used for several years may contribute to children being passively (rather than actively) involved in the learning process.

Children often regard and respect teachers as the source of knowledge, in part because teachers have the major responsibility for evaluating academic progress. Moreover, as children progress through school, they are successively introduced to new learning experiences and material. Children are continually bombarded with new material, and look forward to fresh learning experiences.

Lecture has been a common method of teaching children at the secondary level, in part because it permits materials to be covered relatively quickly. The use of the lecture method is facilitated by the fact that children have relatively homogeneous backgrounds and goals.

In a very real sense, going to school may be thought of as children's jobs. Ideally, they arrive at school fresh, well-rested, and ready to learn.

Andragogy

Andragogy can be thought of as the process by which adults learn. Malcolm Knowles generally is recognized as one of the leading authorities in the study of andragogy. Instructors teaching adults may find it useful to read his books: *The Adult Learner: A Neglected Species; The Modern Practice of Adult*

Education: Andragogy versus Pedagogy; and *Andragogy in Action: Applying Modern Principles of Adult Learning.*

The fact that the term "andragogy" is not listed in many unabridged dictionaries does not imply that it is a new concept. Knowles himself noted in *The Adult Learner: A Neglected Species* that the concept of andragogy existed in Germany in the 1830s, and was being used in the United States during the 1920s. Yet Knowles' work brought attention to andragogy like never before.

Recent research has brought into serious question the very foundations and legitimacy of andragogy. Clearly this research is timely, because the adult education field has expanded over the last three decades in response to technological changes, competition, state laws and regulations, and the like.

Those teaching REEA's Instructor Development Workshops have often asked attendees to make (and explain) lists of how adults differ from children in ways that may affect learning. The basic supposition has been that if children really are different than adults, then those instructing children and adults will find it useful to conduct their classes differently in order to maximize learning,

Although the responses received in Instructor Development Workshops obviously have not been uniform, the *historically-perceived* differences between children and adults are summarized in the remainder of this section.

Andragogy differs from pedagogy in a number of respects. First, attendance at adult educational courses typically is not mandatory. Even though state law may dictate mandatory continuing education requirements, adult students usually have some choices regarding both class subject matter and instructors/schools which they attend. Although time limitations from job or family pressure may influence class choices, in general adults are more likely to attend classes because they want (rather than have) to be there. Students who want to be in class generally are more receptive to learning than those who prefer not to be there.

After age 14 there is a slight but steady decline in the ability to both see and hear. For this reason, distributing study materials in large type and using microphones may aid in learning and effective communication. Reactive time also slows down with age. This does not imply that adults cannot learn, but rather that it may be necessary to use a slightly slower pace to obtain the same degree of learning.

Adults like to be treated like adults, so instructors' attitudes toward students are very important. This is particularly true in classes where the instructor is younger than many of the students, whose ages in real estate classes may range from 18 to 80+. Classes may include heterogeneous students ranging from high school dropouts to Ph.D.s, but all share the common characteristic of wanting to be treated like adults.

Because adults do not like to waste time, instructors should honor this major concern and begin and end class on time. Adults generally are not interested in abstractions, but rather prefer solid information designed to help solve their problems.

Because adults may not have attended class in several years, they often have predictable anxieties. To help relieve these anxieties, at the beginning of the first class instructors should announce such simple concerns as the:

1. schedule for exams and assignments;

2. grading procedures;

3. location of restrooms;
4. location of eating facilities;
5. scheduled times for breaks and meals;
6. parking instructions;
7. reference texts; and
8. other relevant items.

Early announcement of information about these items can relieve students' stress.

Adults differ from children in that they have lifetime experiences on which to draw. Lifetime experiences allow adults to individually decide whether material being presented is useful or useless. The usefulness/useless decision has two important implications. First, adults typically do not accept what is being taught on "blind faith." Second, adults may seek and prefer educational experiences that have immediate application to their professional (or personal) lives -- something that will positively affect the "bottom line" of their business or family activities.

Oftentimes adults exhibit a strong resistance to change. Sometimes their bad (and good) experiences in life have erected a heavy armor of personal prejudices and convictions that are difficult for instructors to penetrate. Many adults have reflected on their lifetime experiences and learned from them. And, because of their lifetime experience, adults often learn from each other. Astute instructors can take advantage of students' lifetime experiences and utilize them as a learning (teaching) resource if they can overcome students' personal beliefs, prejudices and convictions. Building on adult students' experiences, opinions, and practical know-how is a teaching opportunity that generally is not available when instructing children.

Adults recognize that the world is not always black and white. That is, a question often has no single "right" answer, but rather there may be a range of solutions with different consequences. Different solutions may be optimal for different people and business firms, depending on the circumstances that exist and sometimes even on the personalities involved. This "different strokes for different folks" idea also suggests that individual students have different educational needs that should be addressed. Because of these different needs, as suggested in Chapter One, it is important for those teaching adults to become familiar with students' backgrounds.

Adults often have worked all day or all week before arriving in the classroom, so they may be tired. Actively involving adults in learning may provide the stimulation needed to help overcome fatigue, thereby increasing the efficiency of the learning process. Learning by doing -- active involvement in the learning process -- later will be shown to be a significant learning aid.

For many adults, attending class is both a physical and mental obstacle course. Instructors are competing for the attention of students' mental processes. Learning barriers exist where students are thinking about their family and job responsibilities--it's raining or snowing outside, they had to park three blocks away in a bad area, they are going through a divorce, a parent just passed away, two children are in bed with the flu, another child was arrested for the possession of drugs, a business report is due at 8:00 a.m. tomorrow morning, and, to top it off, they are entertaining the bridge club this Saturday evening. These are but a few of the possible barriers to learning that instructors must overcome. They are not unusual barriers, because it is a fact that the desire for additional education often is triggered by a traumatic experience / major life change.

It is well known that many adults doubt their ability to study and learn. Some seek and need help in (re)learning how to study. Closely related is the fear that their low level of knowledge will be exposed for all to see and that they may be ridiculed by either instructors or classmates. Instructors should take appropriate steps to alleviate these fears.

Adult real estate students often seek counseling and guidance in career choices and activities. Some 50-year olds still have not decided what they to do when they "grow up." In colleges and universities, such counseling often is provided by academic advisors. In other settings, instructors may be expected to provide this type of guidance.

Because adults prefer to learn information that is immediately useful, such teaching techniques as discussion, problem-solving, and case studies may be efficient methods of classroom communication (see discussion of teaching methods in Chapter Four). Also, the fact that adults often gauge their own progress rather than being evaluated by teachers via examinations makes adults more receptive to non-lecture teaching techniques.

Many adults are quite comfortable with their lives and are, as previously noted, somewhat resistant to change. In fact, some may actually fear new learning experiences. As an example, some adults may be afraid of computers. At the same time, many adults fear falling behind. Not wanting the "world to pass them by," together with the desire to maintain and/or improve their standard of living, are important factors motivating adults to learn.

Instructors typically have less authority over adult students than they have over children. However, this lack of authority may be more than offset by the fact that adults generally are self-motivated. They have not been coerced to attend class, but rather have well-defined purposes for being there. These purposes may include a new or better job, increased income, solving personal or community problems, or other reasons. Irrespective of their purposes for attending classes, adults typically have immediate needs and seek and expect immediate results. For this reason, many adults will not give a program a second look unless they perceive a personal profit in attending. Stated in a different fashion, the motivation for adult learning can be thought of as consisting of three simple steps, as follows:

1. Learning leads to better job performance.

2. Better job performance leads to recognition.

3. Recognition leads to desired rewards, such as status, income, and standard of living.

Similarities Between Adults and Children

Adults and children are similar in important respects. Both like to be recognized and respected. A well-accepted principle of good management is that people like to be praised. The pursuit of recognition and praise motivates many adults and children to participate in class discussion and learn more, and praising students is helpful in developing rapport between students and teachers. Enhancing students' self-esteem, and making them feel good about themselves, contributes to a good learning environment.

Adults and children also are similar in another respect. In the absence of assigned seating, both tend to sit next to their friends in the classroom. This naturally occurs because people are both creatures of habit and comfortable when sitting next to acquaintances. Sitting next to strangers may make people a little uncomfortable, and put them slightly "on edge." Being "on edge" may increase students' awareness of their surroundings, decrease talking among classmates, and result in closer attention being paid to instructors. Stated differently, taking students out of their comfort zone may facilitate greater learning. For classes that extend over several days, instructors may find it advantageous to periodically change students' comfort levels by moving them around the classroom - so long as such moves are anticipated via expectations set out when classes began.

What Research Suggests About Differences Between Adults and Children

Those who have read the first edition of this book will find the preceding three sections to be highly similar in content to the first edition. A good deal of research has been conducted concerning andragogy since the first edition was written. Often this research was quite sophisticated, complex, and narrow in application. This research might best be summarized by simply noting that the majority of differences between children and adults which andragogy proponents have advocated in fact do not seem to exist.

There have always been a significant number of REEA Instructor Development Workshop participants who argued strenuously that there were no significant learning differences between adults and children. These participants can take pride in the fact that recent research results support their views. As (perhaps) over-simplified illustrations, some children arrive at class just as tired as the adult who has worked all day; similarly, some children have had more experience (and knowledge) about some topics (e.g., the child traveler in a geography class) than their teacher.

At the same time, these research results should not be interpreted to mean that the initial perceptions of andragogy have not been helpful to adult education teachers. In fact, in attempting to take advantage of these initially perceived learning differences between children and adults, teaching techniques were developed and refined which have served instructors well. In short, good teaching is good teaching, irrespective of whether children or adults are in the classroom. Stated differently, teaching techniques designed to take advantage of the perceived uniqueness of adult students often have proved effective aids to improving learning and retention for both children and adults.

But what are the bases of andragogy which help instructors to become better teachers? Knowles summarized them as seven points in *Andragogy in Action: Applying Modern Principles of Adult Learning*. They are:[1]

1. set the climate, including both the physical and psychological environment. Knowles recommends that a full 10 percent of the teaching effort be devoted to setting the climate. In the psychological portion of the environment, he includes a climate of mutual respect, collaborativeness (where students work together rather than compete with each other), mutual trust, supportiveness (where students feel that they are being supported rather than judged), openness, authenticity, and pleasure (i.e., the learning process should be fun).

2. get learners mutually involved in course planning. (This could be done by dividing a class into subgroups, each of which elects a representative to the planning committee).

3. involve students in determining what they need to learn.

4. involve students in developing their learning objectives.
5. involve students in designing learning plans.
6. help students to achieve (carry out) their learning plans. and
7. involve students in evaluating their learning experience.

It is interesting to note that many, if not all, of these concerns can be addressed through the use of learning contracts (sometimes called learning plans or learning agreements). Students are often asked to plan their own learning contracts, and may be encouraged to seek peer review before submitting it to their instructor. Evidence that the learning contract has been achieved often involves the submission of a portfolio (which includes copies of papers, recorded tapes, and the like).

Several additional relevant points can be derived from the relevant research literature of the last several years, including information about learning rates, learning styles, and learning retention.

Learning Rate

For the typical person, the rate at which they learn begins to decline after age 24. However, the ability to learn does not decrease until health starts to deteriorate late in life (beginning at around age 75 for many). This suggests that old dogs can be taught new tricks, but teaching techniques which allow adults a little more time to learn can be expected to work best.

Learning Styles

Not everyone learns the same way. Four distinct learning styles have been identified -- auditory, visual, tactual, and kinesthetic. If classes contained only students with identical learning styles, teaching for maximum retention would be much easier. Since this distribution seldom occurs, many instructors attempt to present materials in such a way that they are providing opportunities for students with each of the four basic learning styles to learn efficiently[2,3]. Although they are discussed separately, many students learn by a combination of two or more learning styles.

Approximately 22 percent of all students are **auditory learners**. (This percentage may differ for various subjects students may study, but the author was unable to find any specific breakdown for real estate students.) Auditory learners learn by hearing, so they basically learn from sounds. Thus, auditory learners may learn by listening to instructors, others, audio tapes and/or films, or by listening to themselves as they recite whatever it is that they wish to learn.

The largest proportion of students learn visually (46 percent). **Visual learners** learn by seeing, so they may learn by reading text books, notes which they have taken in class, or written handouts/supporting materials. They also may learn by viewing films and videos, watching demonstrations, and looking at charts or graphs illustrating relevant principles. Another way that visual learners learn is by writing down their class notes, making lists of important points, and/or by designing flow charts. They also may learn by creating mental images in their minds as they think about information being given to them.

Roughly 20 percent of students are **tactual learners**. They may learn by touching, feeling, performing, tasting, and/or smelling. Handling objects and even writing are examples of the

Figure 2-1: Learning Styles

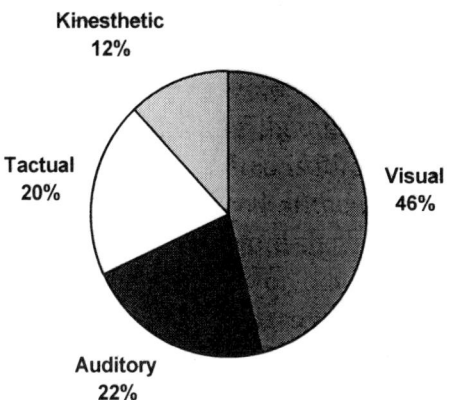

way that their sense of touch assists them in learning. Feelings are also important to tactual learners. They often learn from interpersonal communication, and they will learn more if they are comfortable in the classroom and both like and respect their teachers. An example of tactual learners learning by performing include rewriting their class notes. They also learn most when working/reading at their own pace.

The remaining 12 percent of students are **kinesthetic learners**. Kinesthetic learners learn via hands-on approaches, and physical movement contributes to their learning. Hands on approaches which instructors might utilize effectively with real estate students who learn kinesthetically include field trips, task group discussions, and simulation. Kinesthetic learners learn when they know how to use something and how that something works. They often learn through trial and error, and are performance and project oriented. Case studies also work well for students who learn kinesthetically.

Retention

Learning, retention, and memory are sometimes used interchangeably in the research literature. How much people learn (retain/remember) in various ways can be presented effectively in a "learning pyramid." Research in occupational training indicates that individuals retain about:

10% of what is read
20% of what is heard
30% of what is seen
50% of what is heard and used
70% of what they say
90% of what they say and do

Though the above percentages are only approximations, they do indicate that (A) students learn faster by seeing and hearing than by hearing alone, (B) students learn even faster when doing is added to seeing and hearing, and (C) students tend to remember more of the things they do than the things they are told.[4]

Different sources may show similar (but not identical) information in the form of a pyramid. As an example, the items set out on the next page are combined with the percentage of students who learn by using that item alone.

Instructors really are learning facilitators. They need to employ teaching techniques other than straight lecture if they are to maximize student learning.

Lecture 5%
Reading 10%
Audio-Visual 20%
Demonstration 30%
Discussion Group 50%
Practice by Doing 75%
Teach Others / Immediate Use 90%

THE LEARNING PYRAMID
Source: National Training Laboratories, Bethel, Maine

Summary

Time-tested pedagogical teaching techniques historically used with children have been seriously questioned in recent years. Adult education instructors may, therefore, find it advantageous to use teaching methods other than straight lecture. Provisions should be made to relate to different learning styles (audio, visual, tactual, kinesthetic) through the judicious selection of teaching techniques and audio-visual aids. Remember: learning by doing using interactive processes substantially increases the amount of learning which occurs in *any* classroom, whether it be populated by adults or children.

Exercises for Chapter Two

1. What are the principal learning styles possessed by students? Based on your knowledge of these learning styles, what changes can you make in your current presentations to increase the amount of learning which occurs in your classroom?

2. Identify five topics which you currently teach. Develop methods to teach these topics so that your students learn by doing.

End Notes

[1] At page 14 - 18.

[2] Some of the learning style material set out here was adapted from Ron Brown and Anne Crowley, "Compelling Whys: A Learning Channels Approach," presented to the sixth annual conference of Teaching Economics: Instruction and Classroom Based Research, February 16-18, 1995.

[3] For an excellent short article on learning (processing) styles, see Losapio, Susan, "How Come They Don't Get It?" *REEAction*, p. 6, Dec. 1, 1995.

[4] Hayes, Terry, in a presentation to the 1995 Real Estate Educators Association Annual Conference, citing the *Handbook for Teachers of Adult Occupational Education*, State Education Department of New York, 1977.

CHAPTER THREE

The Learning Environment

Introduction

The classroom environment affects both the rate of learning and the amount learned. In addition to their own capabilities and motivation, the amount which students learn is influenced by at least four separate "environmental" factors. The factors (illustrated in Figure 3-1) include the physical classroom configuration and facilities, other students, written textual materials and handouts, and instructors. These external factors define the learning environment, and each will be discussed in turn.

Physical Facilities and Room Configuration

The optimal classroom layout often varies, depending on class size, the topic taught, and the teaching technique employed. Tables (or other large, flat surfaces) need to be available on which students may both lay written materials and take notes. Failing to provide students with tables makes note-taking physically difficult and causes any lasting benefit from the class to primarily come from students' capacity to remember what was said and/or seen. This is particularly true where substantive handout materials are not provided.

It is well known that the capacity to recall what instructors said significantly declines over time. Thus, the most obvious benefit of providing tables is to encourage note-taking, thereby permitting an opportunity for more, longer-lasting learning to occur. Many adults are out of practice/not adept at note-taking, so anything which instructors can do to facilitate and encourage note-taking will prove beneficial.

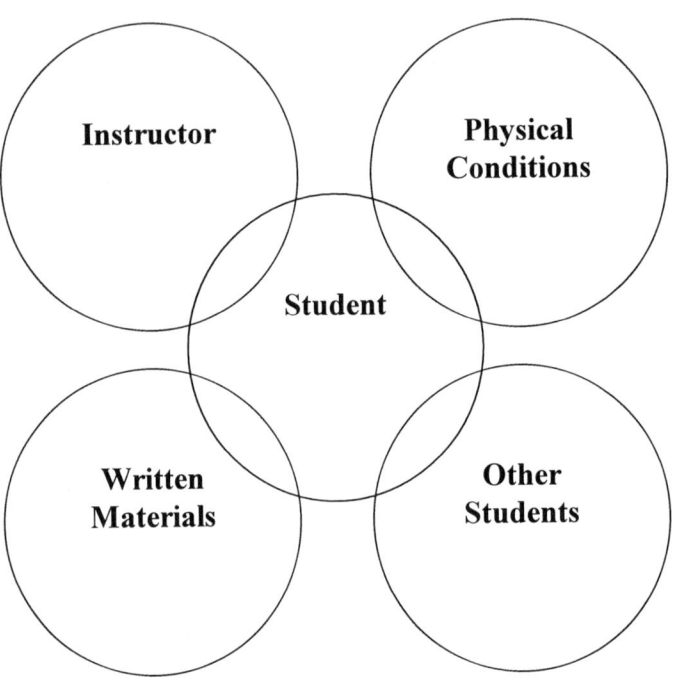

Figure 3-1: The Learning Environment

Two important physical factors are that classrooms be both well-ventilated and well-lit. Light colored or white walls, ceilings, and floor coverings create a feeling of spaciousness and also avoid the depressing, dungeon-like effect of dark surroundings. Outside windows are not essential, and in fact can be distracting in those locations where much is going on outdoors. Unless ventilation is excellent, it usually is best to prohibit smoking in the classroom. Smokers' needs can be taken care of by short but regular refreshment breaks.

The proximity of overhead lighting to reflective (projection) surfaces used for films and overhead projectors is also an important physical consideration. To avoid glare which makes it difficult for students to read the screen, it sometimes is essential that banks of ceiling lights be turned off. If this is not feasible, the offending light bulbs should be removed prior to class.

Many instructors prefer not to use large portable screens because they must be erected some distance from the front wall of the classroom. Depending on the size of the audience, using portable screens may cause student seating to be moved farther back and one or more rows of tables and chairs may be lost from room capacity. Thus, if white or light colored walls are available, using them as the projection surface will increase the effective room capacity.

Some regard podiums or lecterns as physical barriers between students and instructors, and prefer either not to use them or to use them minimally. Both (1) the extent to which instructors rely on notes while teaching, and (2) the type of microphone available may affect the podium use decision. Instructors using overhead projectors may prefer to place the projector on a table 4 - 8 feet long and use the remainder of the space to spread out class notes and resource materials. The relatively low height of tables causes them to be perceived as less of a physical barrier.

When teaching in classrooms that are either unfamiliar or have been used by others recently it is recommended that instructors arrive well before class. Arriving early allows time to inspect (and change if necessary) lighting, podium/lectern availability and location, placement of projection surfaces, and microphone type. Early arrival allows time to determine whether or not everything is functioning properly, and that registration and refreshment tables, as well as room configurations, are satisfactory.

Some possible room layouts are set out in Figure 3-2. At the outset, it should be recognized that the location of doors (not shown in Figure 3-2) affects the optimal configuration of tables and chairs. Doors located near instructors are distracting to both students and instructors when students arrive late and/or leave early, so it is preferable for doors to be at the rear of the room. Also, when capacity crowds are anticipated, the length and width of tables available relative to room width and length may impose practical considerations on what would otherwise constitute an ideal table configuration. But room capacity should not be extended to the point that it has a negative impact on learning. The room capacity will, of course, be affected by local fire code regulations. Moreover, when students are crowded and uncomfortable, learning is adversely affected. Providing comfortable chairs and ample space between chairs (two feet is recommended) may positively affect learning, especially in longer classes. Providing adequate space between chairs is particularly important when students are immersed in working problems, solving cases, or otherwise making extensive use of resource materials.

In general, rapport between students and instructors is better when instructors are physically close to students (but not in their laps!). Often a room set up which is wide but not deep (Part A, Figure 3-2) is preferred to a room which is long and narrow (Part B, Figure 3-2). This preference for closeness to students is particularly obvious among instructors who move around while teaching, as closer proximity facilitates better eye contact and rapport with students. (Note that this basic preference constitutes a challenge for instructors using "master classrooms," as discussed in Chapter 10.)

THE LEARNING ENVIRONMENT 37

Figure 3-2: Some Possible Room Configurations

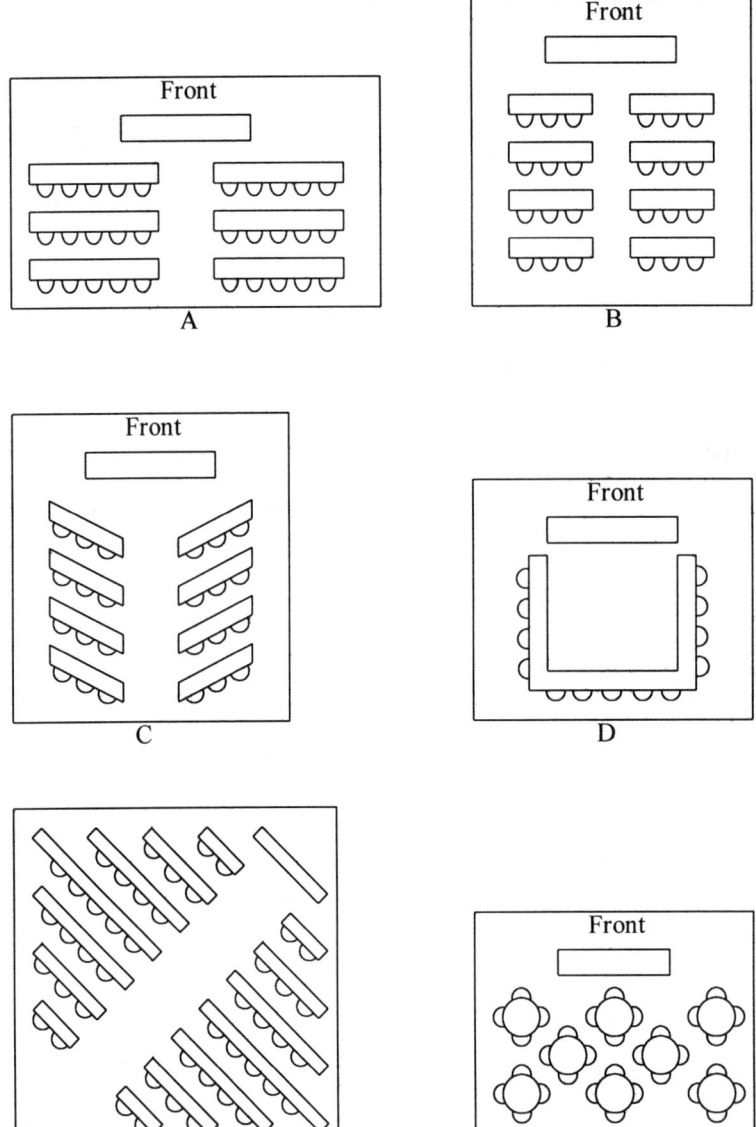

Part C of Figure 3-2 illustrates a "herring-bone" (sometimes called "chevron") type of seating arrangement. When compared to the arrangements labeled A and B in this figure, a major advantage of the herring-bone arrangement is that students' attention is more directly focused on (instructors at) the front center of the room. Also, eye contact with students on the other side of the room is easier than under configurations A and B of Figure 3-2. The opportunity for eye contact with fellow students is particularly important when instructors make extensive use of class discussion and other interactive teaching techniques.

Segment D of Figure 3-2 sets out a U-shaped table arrangement, with students being seated only on the outside of the U. This arrangement works best for smaller groups when eye contact with other students is important. Other room arrangements utilize space more efficiently than the U-shape. Eye contact between students on the same side of the U is still difficult if not impossible. Thus, in some cases a semi-circle arrangement may prove preferable.

Section E of Figure 3-2 illustrates a room arrangement that uses nearly all of the classroom space. This arrangement provides for one corner of the room to be the central focus for instructors and audio-visual equipment. A single, wide center aisle is provided for access. The major space efficiency gained is that fewer tables at the front are lost because of minimum distance requirements between the projection surface and the front row. This arrangement could be modified by "herring-boning" the tables. Those instructors who move around frequently when teaching may find that limiting movement to the small area in the corner plus the center aisle to be somewhat restrictive. Moreover, this room arrangement should be checked to make sure it conforms to local fire code occupancy requirements. If these hurdles are cleared, the Part E type arrangement should be considered when renting space is costly.

Section F of Figure 3-2 shows a room arrangement utilizing round tables. Round tables are very useful where classes are divided into task groups and assigned problem solving/case study responsibilities. In this instance it may be more important for students to have eye contact with (and to be able to hear) other students in their groups than it is to have continuous eye contact with instructors.

Irrespective of the room configuration, students can be encouraged to sit near the front by placing only as many chairs as are needed in the room. This practice also makes checking attendance easier.

When a choice of table cloth color is available, either yellow or white is preferred. Some find blue to be depressing, while red is a power color which can be intimidating.

Occasionally the availability and placement of electrical outlets may affect room arrangements. To the extent possible, all electrical cords should be placed out of heavy traffic areas for both students' and instructors' safety. Taping cords to the floor decreases the possibility of tripping, and is recommended.

Room temperature affects alertness and learning, but it is difficult to find a temperature acceptable to all. The temperature of 68° (Fahrenheit) is recommended, but often body heat from a full classroom requires a 65° thermostat setting to achieve a 68° temperature. An even lower thermostat setting works well for the time period immediately following lunch. Light sweaters or jackets should be suggested for those who find 68° uncomfortably cool.

Other Students As a Learning Resource

Because of their lifetime experiences, students themselves may be a learning resource on some occasions and topics. Students can share new industry developments and explain what courses of action and activities have proven successful for them. In this way, students learn from each other if opportunities for interaction exist. These interactive opportunities include coffee and lunch breaks, general "bull sessions," as well as time spent in the formal classroom.

An obvious way to use students as a learning resource is for instructors to use teaching techniques in which students are actively (rather than passively) involved in classroom activities. Active involvement such as working problems, analyzing case studies, or class discussion encourages student questions and comments from which others can learn. Moreover, student questions and comments can provide new ideas that instructors can formally incorporate into future classes. Instructors should not be intimidated when well-known successful people attend their classes. When such people are directly involved by class discussion (or otherwise), often you can "hear a pin drop" as other students listen carefully to their responses. Successful students have instant credibility with other students because of their well-known successes. Thus, instructors willing to risk giving up a degree of control (to students) may be rewarded with a fantastic educational experience.

Written Source Materials

Obviously, students can and do learn from written materials. Class-related written materials vary from textbooks, to extensive substantive note-taking outlines, to one-page outlines listing the major topics to be discussed. The relative time required to prepare different kinds of handout materials should not dictate the type of materials used. Rather, the decision on the type of materials distributed should be based on an analysis of what is likely to maximize learning. Both the subject being taught and class length influence which type of supporting materials work best.

A weakness of the one-page outline approach is that any new knowledge acquired is directly related to student note-taking ability. At the other end of the continuum, when instructors hand out a copy of every word they intend to say, many students will read ahead, get bored, or otherwise fail to listen. Students may decide to read extensive outline material back at the office and spend the class period daydreaming or working out the numbers for a proposed real estate investment.

Many instructors opt for a middle ground. That is, they may employ a multi-page handout which covers major points but also provides sufficient "white-space" for note-taking. The major points being covered also could be reinforced by in-class problems, case studies, or the like to encourage active participation.

Reliance on textbooks depends on the nature of the course. Textbooks work particularly well for courses extending over several class meetings but often are impractical for shorter classes (particularly those taught in one day). And just because reading textual material prior to class is deemed essential does not automatically mean that timely distribution of textbooks is possible. Thus, especially for one-day classes, distributing substantive, extensive note taking outline materials often is preferable to textbooks.

Instructors

The way instructors teach can stimulate learning. This stimulation can occur in many, sometimes subtle, forms.

First, reasonable instructor movement around the room is helpful in keeping students alert, and also improves eye contact with the audience. Reasonable movement away from the podium (lectern) and the comfort of teaching notes also builds credibility with the students, as this helps them realize that their instructor is knowledgeable about his/her subject. At the same time, unreasonable movement (e.g., rapid pacing back and forth) can be distracting.

Second, instructors asking relevant questions stimulate students to think about how materials apply to their professional and personal lives. Any teaching technique that actively involves students can stimulate learning, especially when such active involvement is with topics which can readily be related to students' personal lives and businesses. Adult students typically are "bottom-line" oriented, irrespective of the subject matter.

Third, nothing causes students to lose interest more quickly than tired instructors. Instructors with high energy levels get students excited about learning. Instructor energy levels are critically important in creating the best possible learning environment. Moreover, instructor enthusiasm is contagious, and is a great aid in overcoming student fatigue. Even such simple ideas as staging food and caffeine intake may help avoid highs and lows in instructor presentations by maintaining a constant (high) energy level. (Note that staging caffeine and food intake also may be important for students seeking to maximize learning.)

Another way for instructors to stimulate learning is to keep the program moving along. When presentations drag, students get bored and their attention dwindles. Often it is better to leave students a little hungry for more knowledge than it is to beat a topic to death in an attempt to cover every possible relevant item.

Finally, periodically changing students' comfort zones may increase their awareness of their surroundings. As noted previously, changing comfort zones puts students a little bit on edge, so occasionally changing student seating may stimulate learning. Remember though, that adults like to know what to expect, so it is a good idea to let them know (at the beginning of class, along with other class ground rules) that periodically they will be moved around the classroom.

Many instructors, and particularly new ones, are nervous prior to and during the early part of class. So long as the "butterflies are flying in formation," this nervousness can be an asset. Just as students learn more when taken out of their comfort zone, instructors on edge often communicate more effectively. Even veteran instructors still feel the butterflies at the beginning of a presentation, and top instructors often have been heard to say that "it is time to quit teaching (a specific topic) when the butterflies cease to be present."

One area in which student evaluations are of particular help is in identifying distracting personal mannerisms exhibited by instructors. Examples of such instructor habits include leaning against the podium (or table or wall), leaving a row of heel marks beneath the black board while leaning against it and standing on one leg (which led to the students' nickname of "the stork"), picking one's nose, continuously jingling pocket change, periodically squeaking chalk across the board, blocking the view of overheads on the projection surface, using "uh" or "O.K." as every third word, and a myriad of other personal mannerisms. Remember that distracting personal mannerisms are really nothing more than bad habits which can be broken with concentrated effort, and their elimination will increase learning for those students to whom they are distracting.

Finally, it is extremely important that instructors communicate the fact that they really care about students. Caring helps to develop rapport, and rapport increases learning.

Summary

Some people believe that instructors' abilities to stimulate learning are God-given and, therefore, teaching is more of an art than a science. But no instructor is perfect, so improvement is always possible. The beginning point for improving instructors' abilities to stimulate students and student learning is to recognize the four principal factors affecting student learning. These factors include the physical facilities, other students in the classroom, the organization, quality, and substantive content of written materials, and the instructors themselves. With proper planning and training, instructors can stimulate learning and improve their classroom learning environment by obtaining the maximum from each of these learning resources.

Exercises for Chapter Three

1. Write down the best idea learned from this chapter.

2. Prepare a list of items that instructors should check when they arrive in the classroom prior to class.

3. Draw an ideal room configuration for instructors utilizing different kinds of audio-visual aids. (Audio-visual aids are discussed in Chapter Nine.)

4. Prepare a list of ways through which students might be utilized as a learning resource for a specific topic which you teach.

5. Outline several techniques that instructors could use in the classroom to stimulate students and otherwise improve the learning environment.

6. List the various kinds of materials that may be handed out to students, noting the advantages and disadvantages of each to both instructors and students (additional information on preparation of materials is presented in Chapter Six). Analyze whether or not the written materials which you distribute could be changed and cause a positive impact on learning.

Figures

Figure 3-1: The Learning Environment
Figure 3-2: Some Possible Room Configurations

CHAPTER FOUR

Teaching Methods

Introduction

Lecture has been the predominant teaching method for many years yet, if learning is to be maximized, many times other teaching methods may be preferred. Recall from chapter two that research in occupational training suggests that students:

> learn faster by seeing and hearing than by hearing alone;
>
> learn even faster when doing is added to seeing and hearing; and
>
> tend to remember more of the things they do than the things they are told.[1]

Today's instructors can choose from several teaching methods which may be used either alone or in combination. These methods include interactive teaching techniques which provide students the opportunity to learn through the process of doing. Both audiences and the topics taught (e.g., prelicense versus mandatory continuing education) affect the choice of teaching method(s), as does the personal skills and preferences of instructors. Even the time of day may influence the choice of teaching methods. For example, teaching techniques which actively involve students in the learning process may work especially well in the evening when students have worked all day and are tired.

Regardless of the teaching method(s) utilized, students appreciate instructors who speak on their level, use readily understandable terminology, are committed to and enthusiastic about the topic, and are willing to listen to and learn from students. Bridges from theory to reality, such as instructors' and/or students' personal experiences, are useful aids to understanding under any teaching method so long as they are directly in point with what is being taught. Simply stated, instructors should consider using CPR (content, practice, and review) on their students when they select teaching techniques for the topics which they teach.

A list of available teaching techniques includes the following:

1. Lecture

2. Discussion

3. Town Hall

4. Task Group

5. Role Playing

6. Case Study/Problem Solving

7. Simulation/Game Playing

8. Field Trips

9. Panel Discussions

The strengths and weaknesses of each teaching technique will now be explored.

Lecture

A survey of adult classrooms across the country likely would show lecture to be used more often than any other teaching method. The major advantage of lecturing is that it permits the presentation of a relatively large amount of material in a short period of time. Lecturing may also be a preferred teaching technique with large audiences when class discussion and interaction are difficult to achieve. If the instructional goal is to present as much material as possible in an allotted time period, lecture likely will be the teaching method chosen.

However, if the instructional goal is for the students to *learn and retain* as much knowledge as possible, other teaching methods, either separately or in combination with lecture, may be preferred. Basically, pure lecture takes away one of the basic resources from which adult students learn - the questions, comments and shared experiences of other students in the classroom. Logically, lecture works best when teaching topics in which the students have little or no background and cannot reasonably be expected to offer experiential insights of significant benefit. For example, lecture may work well in real estate license preparation courses (although some prelicense students can share quality experiences that help others learn).

Unless instructors are dynamic, lecture can be boring. Lecture involves one-way communication. In fact, lecture is sometimes defined (cynically) as a process by which information is transmitted from instructors to students without going through the minds of either!

On the other hand, many instructors use lecture quite effectively in combination with class discussion and other teaching techniques. Often lecture is used to convey basic information, while teaching methods requiring student involvement are utilized to develop new skills.

Enthusiasm about the subject matter is contagious, and teacher enthusiasm is critical regardless of the teaching method employed. Enthusiasm is even more critical for the lecture method of teaching because of the one-way communication involved.

Discussion

The discussion method of teaching permits students to become actively involved in the learning process and typically is used in combination with some other teaching technique, such as lecture, case study, or task group. Discussion provides an opportunity to utilize students' knowledge and background in the learning process, so it is a particularly attractive teaching technique in classes with students who have significant and rich industry experience(s). Moreover, by being actively involved, discussion helps overcome fatigue for those students already tired and not used to sitting in a classroom for long periods. Because discussion involves two-way communication, it also helps ensure that the most pressing student questions are answered.

Discussion requires instructors to exercise sufficient control to keep the dialogue relevant to the principal topic being taught, and to prevent one or a few students from dominating classroom time. Some instructors naturally have the ability to control the direction and depth of discussion, while others acquire it over time. However, the use of class discussion may result in a different set of problems (for instructors) than result from lecture and other teaching methods. For this reason, Chapter Five is devoted to discussion-related and other common classroom problems, and includes some suggested solutions for a few of the more common problems. Remember, superb teachers plan how to conduct class discussion rather than leaving it to chance. They also encourage class participation by making individual students feel good about their comments and questions.

Town Hall

As envisioned in this book, class discussion is used to bring out relevant and important points about a particular topic. On the other hand, the town hall teaching method is more akin to a traditional, New England-type town hall meeting where participants can raise and exchange observations about any issue or topic they wish. The difference between the town hall and discussion methods of teaching may simply be a matter of degree. In a sense, the town hall method of teaching permits instructors to respond to a variety of questions covering a smorgasbord of topics. Some instructors utilize the town hall method effectively, particularly in short classes such as real estate license preparation review. Moreover, a major advantage of the town hall teaching method is that it facilitates coverage of questions which are most pressing to students.

Task Group

The task (break-out, or buzz) group method of teaching involves breaking up the class into small groups, assigning each group the same or a different problem, and asking each group to solve the problem and report their solution to the entire class. Dividing the class into task groups encourages small group class discussion and interaction. In this way it actively involves students in the learning process and provides them an opportunity to learn from each other. Those students who are reluctant to ask questions of their instructors may be more willing to raise these same questions within their task group.

Through the sharing of ideas, task groups can be synergistic. That is, the group output can exceed the combined knowledge level of all participating students because they build on each other's ideas. New ideas often are generated by task groups.

Students periodically can be moved from one group to another, thereby taking them out of their comfort zone (see discussion in Chapter Two) and enhancing the learning environment. Also, the use of task groups is a good way to "break the ice," promote closer student relationships, and broaden student participation in those classes that either are (1) dominated by a few students or (2) composed mainly of students reluctant to enter into class discussion.

Role Playing

Many topics can be taught effectively through role playing. Role playing (usually) requires two or more individuals to "act out" some real world situation. With this background, the responses of the role players may then be used to illustrate important principles which need to be learned. Role playing can be preceded or followed by lecture, and often is combined with class discussion.

Illustrative uses of role playing include techniques by which salespeople may (1) close a sale, (2) obtain sales listings via personal contact, (3) use the telephone effectively, or (4) interpret body language. When properly used, role playing can stimulate both student interest and learning. Real estate salespeople often use role playing to learn new techniques. In this way, any mistakes are made in the privacy of their office rather than when dealing with prospects. Some believe that role playing works best for topics classified as training (e.g., telephone techniques) rather than education.

Students with rich industry experiences are good candidates to participate in a role play. Remember though, that some students are uncomfortable role playing in front of a class unless their roles have been scripted out in advance. A well-done role play requires substantial advance planning.

Case Studies

Typically, case studies involve a written narration of a set of facts to which students are asked to respond. Sometimes students are asked for solutions to specific questions about case studies. In other instances they are simply given the case study, and asked to identify the important problems it presents as well as to prepare alternative solutions to such problems.

The use of case studies as a teaching technique has increased significantly over the years for educational delivery systems ranging from industry seminars to undergraduate and graduate university classes. Although individual students may each be assigned case studies, often case studies are class or task group oriented.

It is sometimes difficult to evaluate the contribution (and understanding) of individual students when task groups are used to attack case studies. One way to partially overcome this grading problem is to ask each task group member to evaluate (grade) every other member of his/her task group.

Case studies encourage active student participation, thereby stimulating learning. They may be equally useful as a learning approach to new problems, or as a device for seeking new solutions to old problems. They bring into play the real world experiences of students, and in this way utilize students as a learning resource. Case studies are useful in breaking down difficult concepts into smaller and simpler components, thereby increasing understanding. Case studies are excellent for relating newly learned knowledge to practical applications.

Simulation/Game Playing

Depending on one's definition, simulation and game playing may be either different or identical teaching techniques. For the purposes of this book, simulation and game playing will be considered to be identical. Taken to the ultimate, simulation/game playing often involves the use of a computer. Because computers are not available in many classrooms, this teaching technique may have a somewhat limited application in many adult classes.

Some may view simulation/game playing as a super case study. To illustrate simulation/game playing, let us divide a class into several teams. Each team could then consider itself a real estate brokerage office. All teams will be given information about the city/real estate market in which they are competitors. This information could include data about the local (and regional, state, and national) economy, the number of sales of houses for various prices in the last quarter, advertising costs, recruitment and training costs for new salespeople, overhead costs and how they change as the brokerage firm changes in size, employment and wage level information for the local economy and major local employers, and other relevant data.

Each brokerage firm (team) would then be asked to independently make several decisions, such as advertising budget, dollars to be spent on recruitment and sales training, and the portions of the marketplace in which they would devote various levels of effort (e.g., what percent of the sales staff would concentrate their efforts on lower-priced, medium-priced, and upper-priced homes).

All of the individual team decisions would then be fed into the computer, and the net result of their actions would be returned through a simulation process. New quarterly data is then distributed to each team. Each team would then look at this new data, together with their performance for the previous quarter, and again make the same business management decisions for the next quarter.

In this way, the "game" would continue for a predetermined number of quarters or periods. The winning team would be the one earning the most income or enjoying the biggest increase in net worth (or market share) over the period of the game.

From an instructional standpoint, the game would be utilized to illustrate the impact of various brokerage firm decisions in a changing economic environment. Additionally, the game would illustrate how each brokerage firm's decisions were interdependent on or affected by the decisions of other firms.

Simulation/game playing actively involves students, and is a particularly effective technique for classes covering advanced topics. It also can assist in maintaining a high level of student interest. A potential disadvantage is that some students may spend so much time trying to figure out how to "beat the game" that they fail to recognize the important principles that the game discloses.

Some instructors may interpret game playing to be different than simulation. The "games" which they use to teach might include crossword puzzles, matching of terms, brainstorming, and games based on popular television quiz shows. Games require substantial amounts of time to prepare, but many students like the active, often competitive, learning environment which games provide. These sort of games often (but not always) are designed to test students ability to recall (rather than apply) information. Others are designed to make students think.

Field Trips

Field trips can be good learning experiences. They often are used in real estate appraisal classes to gather site and other data needed to estimate the value of a subject property. When used in this manner field trips permit students to obtain "hands on" experience in applying basic appraisal principles learned in the classroom. For example, actually measuring a house may be a more efficient way to learn this technique than listening to an instructor explain the measuring process.

Another use of field trips is to promote greater understanding of industry processes. An example might be an excursion to the county court house to learn first hand how to use deed, mortgage, property tax, probate, building permit, zoning, and other public records.

Panel Discussions

Panels are composed of a moderator and a group (panel) of experts. Often the panel focuses on a specific topic, and begins with each panel member briefly presenting his or her views on that topic. The panel then functions essentially as a town hall, with the moderator fielding questions from the audience and directing them to one or more of the panel members.

Questions from the audience may be requested in two different ways. Individuals may stand up and ask their question, using a microphone from the floor if required by audience size and/or acoustics. Alternatively, the audience can be asked to write their questions on note-cards, with program assistants collecting and perhaps even sorting the questions by area of interest. The panel moderator may then direct the sorted questions to the panel member(s) with the expertise to answer.

The success of panel discussions as a teaching device is highly dependent on the skills of the moderator. Moderating a panel is a difficult task. The moderator is responsible for keeping the discussion flowing and directly related to the principal topic. He or she must repeat each question for all to hear, and make instantaneous decisions as to which panel member is best qualified to answer each question. At the same time, if audience participation is low, the moderator must be prepared to personally initiate and ask concise, relevant questions to keep the discussion flowing. Moreover, the moderator must make sure that each panel member has the opportunity to participate. (Panel members may be embarrassed and feel that their expertise is being ignored or challenged if they are not given the opportunity to respond to questions. Additionally, they may feel that their valuable time has been wasted if their sole involvement is a short presentation at the beginning of the program.) The moderator must carefully listen to each question and panel response, and frequently interject short follow-up questions to make sure the initial question was fully answered and that important points were not missed. At the same time, the moderator must be careful not to dominate the discussion because the audience primarily expects to hear from the panel of experts.

Panel discussions often work best on advanced topics, and/or topics of current interest. Examples might be the general economic outlook, or the outlook for changes in mortgage interest rates. Also, panels may be a good choice when industry experts are inexperienced or poor speakers because less speaking expertise is required of panel members than principal speakers.

Summary

Teaching methods available to adult education instructors include lecture, class discussion, town hall, task group, role playing, case study, simulation/game playing, field trips, and panel discussions. Often these methods are used in combination. The background and knowledge level of the class, instructors' abilities and personal preferences, the topic to be taught, and the time of day (energy level of the students) all influence the choice of teaching methods.

Exercises for Chapter Four

1. Write down the best idea you picked up from this chapter.

2. Refer back to the list of teaching methods available. List at least one topic which you teach that could be presented using each teaching method discussed in this chapter

3. Develop a detailed plan for teaching each paired topic/teaching method identified in question number two above.

4. Identify the relative strengths and weaknesses of utilizing the teaching plans and methods set out in exercise number three, and compare these strengths and weaknesses to whatever teaching techniques you currently use in presenting these same topics.

End Note

[1] Terry Hayes, 1995 REEA Annual Conference, citing *Handbook for Teachers of Adult Occupational Education*, State Education Department of New York, 1977.

CHAPTER FIVE

Dealing with Common Classroom Situations

Introduction

This chapter discusses responses available to instructors when dealing with common classroom situations. Some of these situations arise frequently; others occur less often and may never be faced by some instructors. The more common situations range from students who talk so softly that they cannot be heard, to those who continually whisper, to those who would (if permitted) dominate the class. The less common (but equally important) classroom situations include dealing with belligerent students.

The manner in which instructors handle these common (and not so common) situations is critically important. Problem situations handled poorly can damage instructors' credibility, as well as the level of rapport maintained with the class. How common classroom situations are handled has a major impact on the learning environment.

This chapter first identifies some common classroom situations, and then suggests some basic rules to keep in mind when responding to them. The final section suggests some solutions to these problems.

Some Typical Problems

Listed below are several problem situations that might be encountered. Give some thought as to how each situation should be handled while still encouraging class participation and maintaining a high level of rapport.

1. Students who talk so softly that other students cannot hear (their questions or comments).

2. Students who do not quite make a point and whose questions or comments are difficult to interpret.

3. Students who make excellent points, some of which the instructor had not thought about before.

4. Classes that simply will not answer questions and will not enter into discussion.

5. One student dominates the class discussion.

6. The discussion starts to drift away from the main topic.

7. Two students get into an emotional, perhaps even hostile, argument while class is ongoing. In short, they appear ready to fight with each other.

8. One student repeatedly makes "smart aleck" comments in an attempt to become the class comic.

9. Two students continually talk to each other during class, annoying nearby students who are trying to listen to the instructor.

10. One student constantly wants to explain how it (your topic) was done in the state from which he/she has recently moved.[1]

11. One student had a "liquid lunch," and now alternates between being the class comic and snoring loudly.

12. After working an illustrative mathematical problem, a student jumps up and shouts "That's a @@##$$% dumb ^&**& way to do it! You're the worst instructor I've ever seen!"

Some Basic Rules For Handling Common Classroom Situations

Almost all of the classroom situations set out above can be visualized as happening when using class discussion as the teaching technique. As indicated in the preceding chapter (on teaching methods), class discussion is a popular and often efficient method of communicating with adults. Class discussion can be initiated by either students or instructors asking questions of the other. Instructors who ask questions almost always receive answers, although occasionally the responses may be somewhat unexpected. Inexperienced teachers sometimes avoid using class discussion, perhaps in part because of a fear that they may lose control. Yet the use of the straight lecture technique with adults fails to utilize an important source of educational information -- the students with their wealth of real world experiences related to the class topic. Thus, a major advantage of class discussion is that it permits students to actively participate in the learning process.

Fears about using class discussion often can be overcome if instructors will simply think back to times when they were students. Recall the time that a fellow student asked a question and the instructor's response went something like: "That's the dumbest question I've ever heard! If you don't know the answer to that question, you should be back in kindergarten!" During the remainder of the class, how many additional questions did this student ask? For that matter, how many other students later asked questions?

No one likes to be embarrassed in front of a group, so one of the best ways to discourage questions (and class discussion) is to embarrass students. When teachers embarrass students, this creates a lasting negative impression. Moreover, these negative feelings may be so intense that they impede the learning process and foster a bad classroom learning environment.

Often the most important question asked is the first question. Instructors' responses to the first question set the tone and (either negatively or positively) affect the learning environment for the remainder of a class.

Sometimes the first question asked really is a "dumb" question with a very obvious answer. Yet if the students in the class are to be fully tapped as a learning resource, the response to this question is critically important. To avoid embarrassing the student (and discouraging further class discussion), instructors might respond as follows: "That is a good question," and then proceed to explain the answer. The important point is that the best instructors continually attempt to make the students feel good about themselves. In fact, for the classroom instructor **Rule Number One** is to **make students feel good about themselves**.

When students feel good about themselves, they are comfortable with their instructors. Furthermore, students respect instructors who treat them well. A good rapport develops between instructors and students when teachers treat students the way they like to be treated. In a very real sense, Rule Number One i simply an expression of the **Golden Rule** slightly restated: **"D(unto students as you would have them do unto you."**

Rule Number Two is to **maintain control in th classroom.** Adult students are there to learn, and have paid goc money for this privilege. They expect instructors to cover a important topics, and to utilize an appropriate amount of time f each. Additionally, they expect instructors to courteously t firmly handle problems such as those listed at the beginning of this chapter. Keeping Rule Number One and Rule Number Two firmly in mind, the following suggestions are offered for handling the classroom situations set out earlier.

Suggested Solutions to Some Common Classroom Situations

Students Who Talk Softly

We start with the situation where students talk so softly that others cannot hear. Instructors can solve this problem by (1) handing these students their microphone, (2) walking toward these students and cupping their ear in the classic manner in an obvious attempt to hear, and/or (3) by repeating what these students have said so that all can hear. Students are frustrated when they clearly hear an answer but are unsure of the question. Moreover, if they misinterpret what was being asked they may leave class with some incorrect information. This suggests that repeating questions for all to hear is critically important. Failing to repeat student questions for the benefit of others is the most frequent mistake made by instructors utilizing class discussion. If there is *any* question regarding whether or not everyone in the classroom heard the soft-spoken student, the student's question or comments should be repeated.

Instructors may attempt to solve the problem of students speaking softly by simply asking them to "talk louder" or "speak up." If not done tactfully this may embarrass some students. Moreover, typically they initially speak more loudly and then permit their voice to fall to its normal volume. For this reason, asking students to "speak up" does not always solve the problem. Something as simple as asking students to stand while speaking aids others in hearing. Using your own body language to indicate that others are having difficulty hearing (e.g., cupping your ear) often is an efficient response to this common problem.

Students Who Are Difficult to Understand

Students who do not quite make a point and are difficult to follow is the next situation to be addressed. To encourage participation, instructors could restate the student's "good" question, and ask if their interpretation is correct. If this interpretation is not correct, and if instructors still are not sure what the student has asked, one useful technique is to ask the class if someone else can restate the question(s) in a different manner. It may help the students feel good about themselves when instructors accept the responsibility for being unable to interpret questions. Furthermore, quite often one or more other students will be able to assist instructors and others in understanding specifically what was being asked. At times instructors have difficulty interpreting questions because the instructors themselves are on a different "wave length" from that of the class. Such interpretation problems often exist because real estate terminology differs from area to area, so instructors who are "on the road" may find this to be a frequent problem. Using other students as interpretive resources helps overcome this communication difficulty.

Students on Target

When students make a good point, repeat it and emphasize *why* it is a good point. Instructors can phrase the point differently, but should make sure the students understand that their contribution is appreciated. Teachers make contributing students feel good about themselves by telling them they made a "good point," and then illustrating how the students' comments can be applied to important real-world problems.

Non-Communicative Classes

Classes that simply refuse to respond to instructors' questions is another situation which instructors may encounter. One way to break the ice with these classes is to divide them into task groups, assign each group a different question, ask each group to elect a spokesperson and bring back an answer or solution (within a certain time limit) and share it with the class. A variation on this technique is, at the time the spokesperson is to make his/her presentation, to inform the elected spokesperson that he/she has the option of presenting the material or delegating that responsibility to another group member. Breaking the ice also may occur through the use of humor or through practical, in-class problem solving activities. The fact that students are reluctant to participate may be evidence that the instructor did not do a thorough job of breaking the ice when class began.

The Dominating Student

The dominating student is a problem which almost every instructor has faced. Breaking the class into task groups often solves this problem. Instructors can require each group to elect a different spokesman each time they report back with a presentation to the entire class. Alternatively, the domination by one student may dissipate if the instructor is able to involve him/her in the class, such as by asking the student to assist with taping flip charts on the walls. Sometimes it is necessary to announce a coffee break and use this opportunity to visit with the dominant student(s) outside the hearing of others. Instructors might tell the dominating student that they obviously know a lot about the subject and that their contributions are appreciated, but other students need to be given the opportunity to express their views. If at all possible, instructors should avoid embarrassing dominating students in front of the class. Remember, in part students will judge teaching effectiveness by instructors' abilities to control the classroom environment.

Drifting Discussion

It is not unusual for instructors to permit the discussion to "drift" away from the principal topic. This requires some control to bring the discussion back to the main topic. Alternatively, drifting away from the principal topic may signal that it is time to move on to the next subject.

Fighting Students

Occasionally instructors may encounter a situation where two students enter into a very emotional, even hostile argument. In short, they are so upset with each other that they are ready to fight! Hostile students and emotional discussions are tough to handle. Clearly instructors need to take control of the situation in a calm manner. Often hostile situations can be defused and turned into positive learning experiences, perhaps through the assistance of other class members. Instructors might tell the hostile students that they have had "their say," and then ask the rest of the class to identify the critical issues underlying the disagreement. Are there alternative issues that should be explored? Instructors might follow the comments of the non-hostile students with a short summary of the issues and their consequences. At this juncture a judgment must be made as to whether or not to let the discussion continue in a controlled environment, or move on to a less volatile topic. Sometimes the combatants may discover that they really were in agreement, but terminology and interpretation were responsible for the misunderstanding.

Relieving the tension in the classroom often improves the learning environment so, when instructors move from the topic in which the hostile situation arose to a new topic, this may be a good time to inject some humor. Or, humor could be injected at the time of the argument by playing on a popular beer commercial of a few years back. That is, instructors might say "Mr. Jones says it 'tastes great.' Mr. Smith says it is 'less filling.' Class, who is right?"

The Class Comic

Instructors may deal with the problem of "smart alecks" or class comics differently, depending on whether the class is in its early, middle or later stages. Solutions vary from talking to the offending students outside the hearing of other students, to using a mild put-down, to embarrassing the offenders. Embarrassing students should be avoided if at all possible.

Sometimes the "smart" comments can be translated into a positive learning experience. For example, instructors might say "You may have intended that as a joke, but you are making a very important point." This statement should be followed by an explanation of the significant point. Responding in this manner may cause class comics to realize that they can make a positive contribution to the class, and result in any subsequent comments made being serious and substantive in nature. Again, instructors' responses to problems such as this are critical to maintaining a good learning environment.

Whispering Students

Some students annoy others by talking (whispering) while the instructor is teaching. This annoyance may affect only a small portion of the class, but those students being annoyed resent the whispering distraction of their fellow students. For this reason, it is important to solve the problem. Possible solutions include (1) standing near the offenders while teaching; (2) telling the talkers that they are distracting those nearby (at break, and outside the hearing of other students); or (3) separating the offenders by breaking the class into task groups. The latter obviously will be effective, but be sure that the class has already been told to expect to be periodically divided for group work so that the use of task groups is not a surprise. (Remember, adult students prefer to know what to expect, and do not like surprises in the classroom.)

The Recently Relocated Student

This scenario involves one class member continually wants to explain "how it was done" in the state where he/she formerly lived. Not only is this information irrelevant to your class, it may cause them to confuse the rules/practice elsewhere with those in their own community. Talk to the student outside the hearing of others and explain that his/her comments could confuse others. If handled right, this avoids embarrassing the student while making him/her feel good about his/her knowledge level. Be sure you ask him/her to *please* refrain from further comparisons.

The Student Who Has Been Drinking

This situation envisions one student who had a "liquid lunch," and now alternates between being the class comic and snoring loudly. Acceptable solutions again may vary from talking to the offender out of the hearing of other students to giving the offender his/her money back and asking them to leave (making sure that they won't be driving!). Again, as tempting as it may be, generally better class rapport is maintained when offenders are not embarrassed in front of the class. Instructors who move around the room may sometimes solve this problem by standing near the offending student while teaching.

The Combative Student

In this situation, after an instructor works an illustrative mathematical problem, a student jumps up and shouts: "That's a @@##$$% dumb ^&**& way to do it! You're the worst instructor I've ever seen!" When this type of situation occurs in the classroom, it may be difficult to maintain control. Furthermore, instructors may be in such a state of shock that any contingency plan for handling this type of problem may be beyond recall. With this sort of disruption, you can hear a pin drop in the classroom, and the manner in which this situation is handled clearly affects credibility with the class.

Since humor is effective in defusing tense situations, instructors might begin their responses with a statement like "Gosh, I just love it when you're subtle!" or "Obviously, your opinion is different from mine. I can live with that if you can!" Clearly, this is one of the toughest classroom situations faced, so a contingency plan needs to be developed for use if and when such problems arise.

The response to this kind of situation may vary, in part depending on the perception of the offending students' personality. Occasionally, students are encountered who intentionally bait instructors, attempting to make them mad and thereby disrupt class. But unless instructors know that disruption was the students' goal, it might be better to assume that he/she meant no harm, and simply got excited because he/she saw what was thought to be a much simpler solution than the one offered by the instructor.

Thus, one way to respond to student outbursts such as this is to simply ask the shouting student how he (or she) would propose to solve the same problem. If the student's response provides a good alternative way to solve the math problem, tell him/her that the solution offered was equally as good as that offered by the instructor. If still a third method is available to solve the same math problem, show the class the third solution. Teachers can then point out that there is more than one way to solve math problems, and that no one way is the "best" method. Acknowledge the fact that different students may view a particular solution as being easier to understand than other approaches, and students should feel free to use the approach that is easiest for them to understand.

If deemed appropriate, instructors then could inject a little humor into the class by stating that they used to work this problem using the same technique as that suggested by the student concerned. However, they stopped doing so a few weeks ago when a student jumped up and shouted "That's a @@##$$% dumb ^&**& way to do it! You're the worst instructor I've ever seen!"

Summary

The manner in which instructors handle classroom problem situations significantly affects student questions and class participation. Two rules are offered for consideration. First, making students feel good about themselves encourages class participation and helps create a good learning environment. Treating students like you would like to be treated is a good rule to follow. Second, instructors must exercise control over discussion and classroom problems in order to cover all topics in a timely fashion and to maintain credibility with students. It is important to be prepared with a plan of action to handle all of these situations.

Exercises for Chapter Five

1. Write down the best idea you gained from reading this chapter.

2. Develop a list of classroom problems not covered in this chapter.

3. Develop acceptable solutions to the problems listed for question number two. Make sure these solutions are consistent with maintaining control and treating students as you would want to be treated.

4. Develop a list of additional rules that instructors could use while encouraging class participation. Are these rules consistent with the suggestions outlined in this chapter?

End Note

[1] Thanks to Marie Spodek, DREI, for suggesting the addition of this problem and solution.

CHAPTER SIX

Preparing and Presenting Classroom Materials

Introduction

The focus of this chapter is on the preparation and presentation of classroom materials. The reader will recall that Chapter Three discusses the use of appropriate written materials to support the teaching effort. These materials range from the use of a textbook, to substantive note-taking outlines, to a bare bones outline simply listing topics to be covered. It was noted in Chapter Three that textbooks work best for classes extending over several class periods and that the usefulness of bare bones outlines in large part depends on students' (sometimes weak) note-taking ability. Thus, particularly for one-day seminars, the middle ground of providing a reasonably expansive note-taking outline often may constitute the best choice for handout material. This chapter begins by investigating different ways of organizing written handout materials, continues with a discussion of preparing learning objectives, and then turns to some ideas intended to increase the effectiveness of oral presentations. The chapter ends with a discussion of concerns which instructors may have regarding the copyright law.

Preparing to Teach

Written Handout Materials

Hand-out materials should be well written, and be free of both grammatical and spelling errors. The wide-spread availability of word processing software packages for minicomputers has made the goal of error-free handout materials more readily achievable. Word processing also has made it easier to update and improve handout materials.

A disheartening statement to hear from instructors, upon completion of their handout materials and plans for presentations, is: "I sure am glad that task is done, because it was a lot of work and I don't want to do it again!" Obviously, work on outlines and presentations is never done, even when the same subject will be taught time after time. Rather, instructors constantly should seek feedback from students, teachers, and other interested parties in an effort to keep abreast of new industry developments, as well as to improve and update both their handout materials and their oral presentations.

Research

Prior to preparing an outline, instructors should do the necessary research to determine what specific topics should be covered within the general subject to be taught. The research required to prepare handout materials includes reading any assigned textbook(s). It also includes reading other books, articles, and source materials from which parts of presentations are drawn. With respect to mandatory continuing education classes, much of the needed background material is available from local and trade association libraries. Additionally, public agencies and private businesses are useful sources of teaching material.

Also, prior to outline preparation, instructors need to determine the backgrounds and common goals of their students. The readers will recall that methods were suggested to obtain this information in Chapter One.

When courses extend over several class periods, it is essential to first develop a complete course outline, or course syllabus. A course syllabus includes a listing of all major topics to be taught, and often contains a tentative time assignment for each topic. Tentative time assignments help ensure that time allocations will bear some resemblance to the relative importance and difficulty of the topics to be presented. Once the course syllabus has been prepared, attention can then be turned to preparing outlines and other handout material for individual classes and topics. Recognition of the overall learning objectives for a particular class is an essential prerequisite to course outline preparation.

Organizational Alternatives

Note-taking outlines and other learning materials may be organized in at least four different ways. First, the material may be presented chronologically (in order of time). Second, the space-order organizational technique may be logical when specific topics involve different (geographical) "space." A third organizational possibility is topical. Problems-solutions are a fourth organizational technique. Each method of organization will be briefly discussed.

Chronological Outlines. When the subject to be presented has developed over time, understanding may be enhanced by presenting the material chronologically. For example, if the secondary mortgage market is being taught, a chronological outline might begin with the creation of the Federal National Mortgage Association (Fannie Mae) in 1938. Recognition of the role of Fannie Mae in attempting to help lift the housing industry out of the depression may aid students in understanding both Fannie Mae specifically and the secondary mortgage market generally. The Government National Mortgage Association (Ginnie Mae), another major mortgage loan purchaser in the secondary market, came into being in 1968 so it might be discussed next. A historical explanation of the need which Ginnie Mae filled may aid in understanding Ginnie Mae's function and Fannie Mae's redefined role. Instructors could then cover the Federal Home Loan Mortgage Corporation (Freddie Mac) which was created in 1970. Freddie Mac's role in expanding the volume of conventional mortgage loan trading can then be shown to have had a major influence on today's secondary mortgage market.

As another example, assume the topic to be taught is indexed mortgages/deeds of trust. Since fixed interest rates predominated from the 1930's through the 1970's, the presentation might begin with an explanation of fixed rate mortgages. The discussion might then proceed to the legal maximum payment and interest rate limitations (caps) existing for the protection of borrowers (and lenders) when variable rate mortgage loans, renegotiable rate mortgage loans, and adjustable rate mortgage loans successively were authorized for use by changing federal regulations. In this way the instructor could show how indexed loans were introduced and structured for the financial protection of both borrowers and lenders, how caps and indices work, and how they permit a sharing of risks which provide payment and interest rate adjustment protection for both lenders and borrowers. From these two examples, it can be seen that a variety of topics can be taught using a chronological presentation of materials.

Space-Order Outlines. A second major organizational possibility is to use a space-order outline. A good example is real estate appraisal. Appraisers may consider successive data from different geographical areas (space), including national, state, regional, city, and neighborhood factors which impact on the estimation of value decision. In short, this involves the so-called "inverted pyramid" of factors influencing the value of subject properties.

A second example might be teaching the rectangular government survey system. Transparencies can be used effectively beginning with the largest space (e.g., baselines and principal meridians) followed by overlays of successively smaller units of space (e.g., township and range lines; then section lines, quarter-section lines, etc.)

Topical Outlines. The third method of organizing classroom materials is a topical outline. The topical method is frequently used, and simply involves breaking the subject matter to be presented into a number of different but logically related topics. The topics are not necessarily developed chronologically or in terms of space order. Rather, they are simply a series of different topics. Obviously, when topic A serves as a basis for understanding topic B, it is logical to cover topic A prior to topic B. Stated differently, it may make sense to cover simple topics before teaching more advanced material. Thus, topical outlines also represent logical orders for presenting material. Moreover, within a larger topical outline, certain specific topics and subtopics may be organized either chronologically or on a space-order basis.

Problem-Solution Outlines. The fourth basic organizational method available is the problem-solution method. This organizational approach may work particularly well when using the case study and class discussion methods of teaching. In the simplest form, this organizational technique first identifies relevant problems and then offers various solutions to these problems. Such widely-differing topics as equal opportunity in housing to real estate investment analysis could be organized utilizing the problem-solution method.

Outline Format. Licensing law regulators report that the logic of a specific course outline often makes the difference between course approval and disapproval. In the actual classroom, the format of the outline likewise may aid in student understanding. Once the organizational method has been selected, the outline usually proceeds under the following format (using agency law as an example):

I. Major Topic No. 1 (e.g., Agency)

    A. First Subtopic (e.g., Legal Principles)

    B. Second Subtopic (e.g., Practical Problems)

        1. First Sub-subtopic (e.g., Listings)

        2. Second Sub-subtopic (e.g., Deposit Receipt)

            a. e.g., Who represents whom?

            b. e.g., Who pays fee?

                (1) e.g., Commission split

                (2) e. g., Credit for seller

                    (a) e.g., Paid by escrow

                    (b) e.g., Paid outside escrow

II. Major Topic No. 2

    Each successive subtopic (or sub-subtopic, etc.) is indented so that, in a multi-page outline, it is easily related with the major topic (or subtopic, etc.) under which it falls. No number or letter is assigned to a subtopic (or sub-subtopic, etc.), unless these are two or more logical divisions of the material. Thus, it would not be proper to use the following system (because there is no second subtopic to enter as Item B).

I. _____

    A. _____

        1. _____

        2. _____

II. _____

Rather, a better way of organizing the material would be:

I. _____

    A. _____

    B. _____

II. _____

        Developing note-taking outlines in this fashion helps instructors organize their thoughts so that all materials will be presented logically, thereby making it easier for the students to understand what is being taught and how one topic relates to another.

        Some instructors find it difficult to sit down and immediately draft a logical outline. One way to overcome this difficulty is for instructors to place all of their thoughts on note cards, and then organize these note cards into a logical working outline. Other instructors may simply construct a T-chart on a page, listing the principal topics on the left-hand side and important sub-topics on the right-hand side. By preparing and ordering T-charts, essentially the same organizational objective is accomplished as with note cards. Also, the availability of computers and word processing software programs makes it easy for instructors to first enter all of their thoughts on important topics and later reorder the material into a logical presentation framework.

Learning Objectives and Lesson Plans

Although many adult education instructors do not use formal lesson plans, clearly lesson plans can be helpful in planning and presenting materials. Basically, a lesson plan simply involves setting learning objectives (what the instructor hopes to teach) for each "lesson," and outlining teaching methodology by which these learning objectives will be accomplished. Determining what the students need to learn is particularly important for beginning instructors, as it helps ensure that irrelevant materials will not be presented. Being familiar with student backgrounds and goals aids instructors in determining appropriate learning objectives for their lesson plans. In recent years, several real estate regulatory agencies charged with approving and/or disapproving mandatory (continuing and other) education classes have begun requiring learning objectives to accompany course outlines submitted for approval.

Presumably, instructors have a set of learning objectives which they hope to accomplish for every class they teach. Since adult students like to know where they are going, the instructor's learning objectives should be clearly communicated to the class. Students enroll in class for specific reasons, so instructors need to relate their teaching as closely as possible to students' questions, problems, and needs. When developing learning objectives, instructors will find it helpful to ask themselves these simple questions,

1. Why are students attending this class?

2. What do students hope to gain from attending this class?

3. How adequate are the students' backgrounds for this class?

Recall that methods for obtaining the information needed to answer the third question were discussed in Chapter One.

"Learning objectives are concise statements which describe measurable behaviors the learners will be able to perform upon completion of the course."[1] If no examination is required at the end of the course, the learning objective can be constructed quite simply by identifying both the members of the audience (e.g., real estate licensees) and the behavior which they will be able to exhibit after taking the course. As examples, after taking this course, the licensee will be able to:

1. qualify the buyer for home purchase, using the same qualifying ratios as those employed by local mortgage lenders;

2. compute the PITI for a specific property; and

3. explain the closing statement to his/her client.

Note that the behaviors which students will learn are both observable and measurable. If the success of a teaching effort is to be judged, it is important that all learning objectives be measurable.

Learning objectives may be written at three different levels as instructors progress from basic to more advanced topics. Beginning with learning objectives at the basic level:

1. "... the learner is expected to know something. Learning objectives at this level usually include behaviors such as list, describe, recall, recite, identify, and locate."

2. "The second learning level is comprehension. Learning objectives which expect the learner to demonstrate comprehension of the material covered usually include behaviors such as translate, interpret, summarize, explain, compare, contrast, classify, diagram, and illustrate."

3. "The third level is application. Behaviors one might target in this category include solve, predict, create, construct, compose, estimate, and measure."

Knowing how to prepare learning objectives not only assists instructors in achieving regulatory approval of new courses, but also helps to prepare courses of high quality.

The Presentation

Irrespective of the handout materials used and the instructional methods chosen, all oral presentations are composed of three basic parts -- the beginning, the middle, and the end. Each of these parts is essential for instructors to be successful in the classroom. Educators sometimes say that, in a class presentation, "you should tell students what you are going to tell them, tell them, and then tell them what you told them." This is a good rule to remember and follow.

The Beginning

Some instructors essentially begin a presentation as follows: "This is good stuff, so you should know it." Their statement may be true, but adult students usually make up their own minds about whether or not the material being presented is really important to them. When adults are told that they should know something without being told why, they may not "tune in" their instructors until well into the presentation. In the meantime, these students may have missed some important ideas and materials. For this reason, it is imperative that instructors immediately gain students' attention at the beginning of a presentation. This is accomplished by using a "hook."

A "hook" is an effective attention-getter. For example, if instructors are teaching the state real estate license law, they might use a hook such as this: "Are you aware that there are 41 different ways that you can lose your real estate license?" Or, if instructors are teaching a session on anti-trust and real estate brokerage, they might start by saying "Are you aware that real estate boards and real estate brokerage firms have paid out over $30 million (or whatever the appropriate figure is) over the last twenty years as a result of anti-trust lawsuits? Anti-trust lawsuits are avoidable, and in this seminar some ideas will be presented on how to avoid them."

Hooks are important! Instructors should always use them so that they will immediately obtain students' attention. If the class has several different topics in it, instructors will find it beneficial to use a hook for each new topic. Otherwise some students may view a particular topic as "filler" presented only to fill out the allotted time, and permit their attention to wander and miss the opportunity to learn important information. Often it is the judicious use of high quality hooks which constitutes the essential difference between an average and an excellent teaching performance.

When beginning presentations, instructors should never apologize for their lack of preparation. First of all, professional instructors should always be well-prepared, so apologies should never be necessary. Second, if instructors really are unprepared, many students will recognize it anyway before the presentation is completed. Third, students could interpret a statement about lack of preparation as indicating that instructors do not consider either their students or this presentation important enough to justify preparation time. In turn, this may lead some students to "tune out" instructors until well into the presentation, missing out on some important points in the meantime.

The first few minutes of a presentation are the most important because they set the stage for what follows. This portion of the presentation should be made in positive terms, and instructors should clearly demonstrate that they know exactly what they are going to say throughout the class. Instructors should never make excuses for their subsequent presentation, even if they are ill. In fact, one mark of true professionals is that they do their job well even when they may not feel like it.

A "road map" should be presented at the beginning of every class. That is, adult students want to know where they are headed and what they will be able to accomplish by successfully completing the course. Most students do not like surprises, so students should be told up front that, for example, from time to time they will be moved around and assigned work in task groups. This information is, pure and simple, part of the needed road map.

The Middle

In a very real sense, the "middle" of a presentation contains the substantive material that instructors are putting forth. The "middle" may contain important problems, as well as ideas for their solutions. It is important that the illustrative examples used by instructors be good ones. Illustrative examples need to be both clear and relevant to clearly defined learning objectives. Moreover, instructors should both consciously and constantly strive to achieve their learning objectives/teaching goals. It should be kept in mind that teaching goals do not include making the instructor look good.

Important substantive principles may require two or three examples to be fully understood and to assure communication with students. Instructors should start with simple examples before moving to more complex ones. Also, instructors communicate more effectively when they begin with examples which are familiar to and/or have practical application for students. To make the program flow, smooth transitions (sometimes called bridges) should be planned and used to move from one topic to another. Smooth transitions are another hallmark of excellent instruction.

Materials need to be presented in a logical sequence to enhance the efficiency of the learning process. And, when teaching adults, instructors usually will want to provide students with opportunities to interact with each other as well as with their teachers. Do not forget that students themselves are an important source of information from which the entire class can learn!

It is important to appeal to different learning styles throughout the presentation. And keeping topics (or subtopics) to less than 20 minutes in duration will help avoid "attention span deficit." Something as simple as introducing each new topic with a graphic, showing a "cartoon of the day," and/or emphasizing a "quote of the day" are effective techniques that may aid learning.

"Chunking" information together is another good technique that helps students remember/learn. As a simple illustration, if the last four digits of a telephone number are 3293, more people will remember this number if it is presented in two "chunks" (32 and 93). Another example of chunking is to use the "Las Vegas rule" to help students remember how many square feet are in an acre (43,560). Summing the first two digits yields a good number to have in Las Vegas (i.e., 4+3=7), likewise adding the second two digits gives another good Las Vegas number (i.e., 5+6=11). But the odds are in the house's favor, so those who play too long will end up with zero. Thus, 7+11+0 helps students remember that there are 43,560 square feet in an acre. Using a visual aid to show 7+11+0 below the correct square footage of 43,560 while talking through the Las Vegas rule appeals to at least two learning styles (visual and auditory). Do you have a feel for teaching to these and other learning styles?

Throughout the "middle," remember that adults are not used to sitting in the classroom. To keep their minds from wandering, it may be helpful to periodically remind students how the material being presented affects their business and why it is important to them (i.e., use hooks often). Instructors may want to emphasize the most important points by presenting them in several different ways and contexts. Moreover, instructors should not be afraid to repeat important points because learning often occurs through well-spaced and well-planned repetition. Also, teachers should keep in mind that motivation and learning go together. Reminding students that they can take home the information taught and use it to improve their bottom line is an important learning motivation in and of itself.

When instructors are having difficulty communicating, some may have a tendency to blame this communication problem on a "slow" class or a group of "resistant" learners. This is somewhat akin to a repairman blaming the problem on the fact that a machine is complicated and moving on to the next job without repairing the machine. Obviously, repairmen are expected to isolate the problem and make the needed repairs. By analogy, this suggests that, irrespective of the past effectiveness of teaching techniques, instructors should not be afraid to try new approaches when standard approaches are not working. In a very real sense, each class has its own "personality" because of differences in students, student backgrounds, and even learning styles. Superior teachers will recognize these differences and seek new and different ways to communicate important concepts, rather than blaming communication problems on their classes. At the same time, remember that the ultimate responsibility for learning is on the student rather than the instructor. Galileo is reported to have said "You cannot teach a man anything. You can only help him discover what is within himself."

Occasionally instructors may not prepare sufficient material to fill the allotted time. Unless mandatory continuing education time requirements dictate otherwise, usually it is a good idea to stop after all prepared materials have been presented. Students usually recognize when unrelated or "filler" information is being presented, and the presentation of "filler" material often detracts from otherwise superb teaching efforts. This problem can be avoided by remembering one simple rule: It is better to come to class with more material than can be presented than it is to run short.

Monotone presentations are a good sleeping pill. Thus, it is important for instructors to vary the volume, pitch and pace of their voices to retain attention. As discussed earlier, when instructors keep their energy at high levels, they are less likely to revert to speaking in a monotone. Also, occasional pauses can help emphasize important points. Moreover, instructors with weak voices may need to use microphones as discussed in Chapter Nine.

The Ending

It is at the "end" that instructors tell students "what they have told them" by repeating the major points made during the presentation. These closing comments should give students both direction and confidence as they complete a class. The direction given to students may simply be that if they implement the plan of action given them by their instructors, they will be successful in their subsequent business and personal activities.

The "ending" should reinforce what has been taught. When adult students realize that they really do understand the major points taught, they will be confident that they can go home and apply what they have learned. Student realization that "they can do it" is what reinforces and builds confidence. While some would claim otherwise, student realization that they understand important and relevant principles is a more important and longer-lasting source of confidence for many students than inspirational (motivational) speeches.

Instructors and Copyright Law

Among other things, copyright laws are designed to protect authors of written (and other) materials from piracy and unfair use of their work product by others. Ideas, concepts, processes and systems are among the items that cannot be copyrighted, but the written expressions of such ideas, concepts, processes and the like can be copyrighted. Because they are the instructor's (author's) written expressions, textbooks, outlines, test bank questions and handout materials prepared by instructors may be copyrighted and protected from copying and use by others.

Today, no formal filing procedures are required to create basic copyright protection. Rather, instructors' written (or taped) material is automatically protected by copyright law from the moment their pen leaves the page. Copyright protection permits the author of copyrighted material to seek recovery of actual financial damages caused by unauthorized uses of such materials by others.

On the other hand, filing written materials with the Register of Copyrights entitles the owner of copyrighted materials to recover statutory damages (e.g., $70.00 per distributed copy) from those using materials without the copyright holder's permission. Clearly this provides substantial protection for authors and leads many instructors to formally obtain a copyright on their personally-prepared written instructional materials.

To achieve protection from copyright laws, authors should give notice that published materials are copyrighted. This may be done by inserting at the start a short statement (notice of copyright) containing (1) the name of the copyright owner, (2) the year the material was first published, and (3) the fact that the material is copyrighted. A copyright notice meeting these three requirements might be: Copyright 1995 by Don Doe. Often the person preparing written teaching materials is the author, but copyrights may be transferred by agreement to publishers and others.

In a very real sense, using copyrighted materials without permission is stealing the copyright holder's property. Obviously, if real estate instructors spend months developing teaching outlines and handout materials for a particular seminar or course, they will and should be concerned if another instructor obtains a copy of their materials and begins using it as his or her own without permission and without compensation.

For more information about copyright protection and procedures, circular R-1 can be obtained from:

Register of Copyrights
Library of Congress
Washington, D.C. 20559

Summary

The preparation of handout materials, lesson plans, and oral presentations constitutes the nucleus of adult education instructional activities. Moreover, how well materials have been prepared and presented are important factors used by students to evaluate how effectively instructors teach.

Research is the first step in preparing and presenting educational materials. Handout materials and oral presentations can be organized in at least four different ways - chronologically, space-order, topically, and problem-solution. Irrespective of the type of outline utilized, measurable learning objectives should be prepared for all material presented.

Presentations may be simply and logically divided into three parts - the beginning, the middle, and the ending. Hooks should be used in the beginning and when new topics are introduced to immediately obtain students' attention. The middle contains the bulk of the substantive material being taught, and it is here that careful attention should be paid to both teaching techniques and learning styles. The ending reviews and reinforces what has been taught, and is an important source of confidence to students that they can effectively use learned materials in their professional and/or personal activities.

Exercises for Chapter Six

1. Write down the best idea gleaned from this chapter.

2. Prepare brief outlines of topics that can be taught using, respectively, the chronological, space-order, topical, and problem-solution organizational techniques.

3. Prepare a beginning (hook) for each topic outlined under question number two.

4. Prepare a student confidence-building ending for each topic outlined under question number two.

5. Prepare a list of learning objectives for each topic that you teach, using the rules set out in this chapter.

6. Prepare a list of topics which you teach for which "chunking" might improve learning/retention.

End Note

[1] Hayes, Terry, "Writing Learning Objectives with Regulatory Appeal," *REEAction*, January-February, 1995, p. 4. The remainder of this section on learning objectives draws heavily on this article.

CHAPTER SEVEN

Effective Use of Humor

Introduction

Some instructors are funny. Others are not. Most would agree that there is nothing worse in a classroom than instructors who try to be funny but are not. On the other hand, humor helps hold students' interest, and interested students learn more. Moreover, humor can be used effectively to emphasize important points, as well as to help students remember. Thus, it is important to achieve an acceptable balance of humor and substantive remarks.

The Two Extremes

At one extreme, there are instructors who primarily function as entertainers. Students may leave class with their sides sore from laughing. The students leaving class can be heard to make such comments as:

"Boy, wasn't he funny?"

"That's the most fun I ever had in a continuing education class!"

"That lady missed her calling in life. She should have been a night club entertainer!"

The written evaluations are similar. A sampling might be:

"Most enjoyable class I ever attended!"

"Super instructor! Class really went by quickly."

"Worst instructor I've ever seen. I didn't learn anything at all."

Whoa! The last comment makes an important point. Most adults attend class because they want to learn something which contributes to their goals, preferably immediately. Even the students who left class laughing may change their minds about the effectiveness of humorous instructors after they return home and have time to reflect on their classroom experience. This change in evaluation may be clearly reflected if post-class evaluations are conducted 30-60 days after class ends. Short and simple, many students feel cheated when a presentation is mostly humor and very little substance. It is for this reason that instructors seeking long-term repeat business need to guard against excessive use of humor.

At the other extreme are instructors who never use humor. Already tired students may find it hard to stay awake in their classrooms, particularly if all materials are presented in a lecture format with a dull monotone voice. Thus, even though the substantive materials being presented are relevant, students who are tired, disinterested and bored may well miss important points which would have been useful to them.

The Middle Ground

The two extremes of no humor and all humor suggest that a middle ground exists that will result in more substantive learning. In particular, occasionally using humor to emphasize important points helps students remember these points. Moreover, the most effective humor often is directly related to the material being presented. The following observations are offered.

Class Size

It is easier to make people laugh in a large class than in a small one. Each class has its own personality, but in large classes humor may be almost synergistic. Some people just do not laugh out loud unless others are also laughing.

Slapstick Comedy

Slapstick comedy often is not very humorous unless the audience is already loosened up and thinks everything is funny. Also, unless the slapstick comedy is in some way related to the substantive topics being taught, the class may well feel cheated if too much time is devoted to it.

Canned Jokes

Canned jokes often backfire. The funniest remarks made in class often are spontaneous, perhaps even one-liners. These spontaneous one-liners naturally flow out of the interaction between instructors and students.

Smiling Instructors

When instructors smile and laugh, it frequently is contagious. A reasonable amount of humor helps break the ice with classes, and is an important aid in retaining students' attention.

Off-Color Humor

Some students will be "turned off" when instructors either tell off-color jokes or make a student the butt of their jokes. Just because many students laugh does not mean that others were not offended. Because of the potential loss of credibility with some students, often it is best for instructors to make themselves the butt of their jokes. In a similar fashion, put-downs, ethnic humor, sexist humor, and the like should be avoided. In fact, discrimination laws effectively detail those types of humor which should not be used. This suggests avoiding the use of jokes based on such factors as race, religion, color, country of national origin, sex, age, and physical/mental handicaps.

Rapport and Credibility

The use of humor may do nothing more than show that instructors do not take *themselves* too seriously. But even the recognition of this fact may be important in establishing rapport and credibility with an adult class. Remember, the use of humor need not indicate that instructors do not take their *subject* seriously.

Memory Hooks

Humor may be used as a "memory hook" (sometimes called a "mnemonic device") to assist students in remembering important facts. To illustrate, suppose instructors are teaching how to calculate percentages in basic mathematics. One instructor, recognized with national awards, uses the (Julie) Garton-Good Gozinta theory to teach percentages. Her theory states:

> The big goes into (Gozinta) the little, or

The bottom goes into (Gozinta) the top.

Another use of a humorous memory hook suggested by John Reilly, DREI, might be as follows:

If you die in California and are buried in Maine, that is dying *interstate*. However, if you die without leaving a will, that is dying *intestate*.

Acronyms

In a similar fashion, humorous acronyms can be developed to help students recall important characteristics and lists of information. For example, the joint tenancy type of co-ownership could be present under the common law only if the four unities of time, title, interest, and possession were simultaneously present. Another basic characteristic of a joint tenancy is that a right of survivorship exists, thereby permitting surviving co-owners to accede to a deceased co-owner's ownership interest without the necessity of extensive probate proceedings. Students may remember these important characteristics of a joint tenancy through the use of the acronym TTIPR (teetipper) - time, title, interest, possession, and right of survivorship.

Rhymes

Humorous rhymes are another way that instructors can teach important points. To illustrate, in law it is well known that the use of the suffix "or" or "ee" identifies someone as either transferring or receiving something. Yet many students have difficulty identifying which party (borrower or lender) is the mortgagor and which is the mortgagee because they tend to look at who transfers and receives the money (rather than who transfers and receives the mortgage instrument). Moreover, humorous rhymes can help students remember that mortgagors (borrowers) transfer mortgages to the mortgagees (lenders). Two commonly used humorous rhymes are:

> It is better to be
> the mortgagee;
>
> and
>
> Simon Legree,
> the mortgagee.

Puns

Some instructors make effective use of humorous puns in teaching. To illustrate, if a person dies owning real estate, has no heirs and does not leave a will distributing his or her realty, ownership of the realty transfers to the state via the process of escheat. Instructors may state that this is easy to remember because es / *cheat* deals with the government!

Puns are sometimes described as the lowest form of humor, so excessive use of puns (or any other type of humor) should be avoided. Instructors want to be remembered for excellence in teaching, rather than as punsters.

Cartoons

Some instructors make effective use of "cartoons" shown on a projector to illustrate important points. To be of maximum effectiveness (and as noted in Chapter 9) students should be able to recognize the point of the cartoon within two to three seconds. Instructors may also use cartoons to regain the attention of their classes at the end of refreshment breaks. (But if using cartoons developed by others, instructors must be careful to avoid violation of copyright laws, as discussed in Chapter Six). Also, many books containing humor for speakers/instructors are available in local libraries and bookstores.

Summary

It is not essential for instructors to be funny. However, letting the students know that instructors have a sense of humor is important. Instructors should never be afraid to laugh with the class (but never at the class) when something funny happens -- even if it was the instructor's mistake that was funny. Teachers who laugh at their own mistakes are simply showing the class that they are human.

An excellent use of humor is to help students remember major points. But off-color humor (including humor based on race, color, religion, country of national origin, age, sex, sexual preference, marital status, handicap, and receipt of public assistance benefits) should be avoided.

Exercises for Chapter Seven

1. Write down the best idea that came out of reading this chapter.

2. Classify recently heard humor by type (e.g., puns, rhymes, acronyms, etc.).

3. On a scale of one (lowest) to ten (highest), rate each specific use of humor identified in exercise number two.

4. Ask students and other instructors to rate each specific joke/use of humor that you use on a scale of one (lowest) to ten (highest)

in the same fashion as exercise three. Were there any significant differences in ratings between exercises number three and four? Does this exercise provide insight as to which type of humor you can use most effectively?

CHAPTER EIGHT

Dress and Body Language

Introduction

Students often form impressions about instructors on the basis of dress and/or body language. Both dress and body language are a form of nonverbal communication, and affect instructors' credibility. For this reason, it is important for teachers to give some thought to both how they dress and how students may interpret posture and body movements. Moreover, instructors astute at interpreting body language can use students' posture and body language to improve their teaching performance.

Dress

More instructors make the mistake of underdressing than overdressing. Wearing open-necked shirts, excessive jewelry, or similar informal attire may be regarded as unprofessional by some. On the other hand, wearing a business suit is universally acceptable. (An exception in some localities may be pantsuits worn by women instructors.) Instructors can always "dress down" by taking off their coats (and, for men, ties) if they feel it is demanded for particular audiences. On the other hand, it is difficult to switch to dressier apparel once instructors are in class. Inappropriate dress can detract from an otherwise superb teaching performance.

Additionally, some students simply expect instructors to be dressed in a suit, and may initially question underdressed instructors' credibility. Arguably, even if only one student has this viewpoint, it still is worthwhile to be well-dressed. It is sometimes said "You are what you wear." To proponents of this view, John T. Malloy's *"Dress for Success"* and *"Women's Dress for Success"* (Warner Books) are books well worth reading.

Gaudy jewelry, plastered on make-up, and flashy clothes worn by instructors are distracting to some students. Any distraction on the part of instructors impedes learning, so conservative dress often is preferable. Many instructors believe it is best to always wear a suit-coat, removing it only when the air conditioning system breaks down on a hot day. At the same time, some audiences feel more comfortable when instructors dress similarly to students. Thus, acceptable dress varies among audiences and regions of the country. (Speaking at a convention in Hawaii is an example.) This suggests that instructors should know their audience well before selecting what to wear.

But notwithstanding the previous discussion, appropriate dress does change over time. When in doubt, a good course of action is to visit leading local clothing stores to learn their view on trends and appropriate dress.

Instructor Body Language

If instructors lean against the lectern or wall and appear bored, it should not be too surprising to discover that their students also are bored. Clearly, eye contact, posture, maintaining a high energy level, and reasonable movement around the classroom all affect the quality of the learning environment. Instructors chewing gum, smoking cigarettes, and drinking coffee while teaching is distracting to some and projects a less than professional image.

In recent years, much has been written and said about the interpretation of body language (and, more generally, neurolinguistics).[1] Much of this discourse has been written for managers and salespeople, so instructors interested in body language have had to read between the lines to glean information useful in classrooms. This chapter attempts to outline a few observations on body language important to instructors. The following are interpretations which students might make about instructors' body language.

Instructors Who Sit Continuously

Unless instructors are sitting because of an obvious physical disability, students may interpret sitting as indicating a tired and/or bored instructor. Students also may recognize that it is easier for them to take over control of the class when instructors are sitting rather than standing.

Instructors Who Continually Touch Students

Because such touching could be both offensive and misinterpreted, it is probably best to avoid such touching.

Pacing Instructors

Instructors who continually pace back and forth across the room virtually wearing a path in the carpet can be distracting. On the other hand, reasonable movement around the classroom aids in maintaining attention and control.

Instructors Who Lean on the Lectern

Instructors who continually slump over the lectern run the risk that students may interpret such slumping as boredom or tiredness, either of which may be contagious with the class.

Smiling Instructors

Instructors who frequently smile may lead students to believe that they love their subject and enjoy teaching. Smiling helps retain students' attention, and helps students realize that it is fun to learn something new and useful.

Intimidation and Safe Space

It is well known that persons standing and talking to others often stand at an angle (rather than directly facing the second person) when they feel intimidated or threatened. This information is useful to classroom instructors. To illustrate, suppose students are seated at tables and working an assigned in-class problem. The instructor is moving about the classroom, giving assistance to students experiencing difficulty in working the problem. To avoid intimidating those students needing help, at least three possibilities present themselves.

1. When standing across the table from students being assisted, instructors could stand at an angle rather than directly facing the student. This minimizes the chances that students will be intimidated.

2. If a vacant chair is available beside students needing assistance, instructors might ask "May I sit here?" Once seated, instructors might ask "May I lay my book here?" The basic idea is that everyone has a certain "safe space,"

and may feel intimidated when their safe space is invaded. Thus, the two questions suggested assist in minimizing intimidation of students.

3. In a crowded classroom, it may be necessary to remain standing and lean over students' shoulders when giving assistance. If so, it is helpful to know that some students feel more threatened when instructors lean over the shoulder of their hand used for writing. Thus, it may be preferable for instructors to lean over the left shoulder of right-handed persons, and vice versa. This practice also makes it easier to see what students have been writing.

Student Body Language

Just as students may interpret body language, instructors may use their interpretation of students' body language to make adjustments in their presentations. Some illustrations are:

Smiling Students

Hopefully, if the majority of students are smiling this provides some evidence that these students are enjoying learning. On the other hand, smiling students could indicate that:

1. the instructor has lost control of the class and the students are smiling at jokes being told in different corners of the room,

2. the teaching effort is so bad that students are laughing at the instructor; or

3. male instructors are teaching with their fly open. (Remember the alphabet, or ABC-XYZ rule - Always Be Careful - eXamine Your Zipper!)

Instructors in tune with their classes will know and/or learn why students are smiling.

Frowning Students

If several students are frowning, this may indicate that:

1. students do not understand the concept being presented;

2. students cannot see the material presented on the screen, blackboard, or flip chart;

3. students cannot hear what is being said; or

4. other students are distracting attention away from instructors.

In any event, the instructors should, through observations or questions, learn why students are frowning, and adjust their presentation to turn the frowns into positive learning experiences.

Students are Tilting Their Heads

Tilting heads often suggests difficulty in hearing, so the use of microphones, speaking louder, and projecting one's voice toward the class may help more learning to occur.

Disinterested Students

Suppose several students are sprawled out in their chairs, no one is taking notes, and some students have laid their heads on the table. This likely indicates that students are tired and/or bored. This may signal that it is time to move on to a fresh topic, to inject some humor, for instructors to raise their personal energy level, or to take a break.

Checking Comprehension

When instructors check for comprehension by asking the class "Does this make sense?" the response is a shaking (or nodding) of several heads. Although sometimes this movement is very slight, it represents an almost involuntary response which helps instructors to know whether or not additional explanation is needed. Particularly when a large number of students give the same response, body language is a useful cue to instructors.

Summary

Body language provides signals from instructors to students, and vice versa. Instructors should avoid distracting dress and mannerisms, because such distractions impede learning. Also, instructors should avoid body language which intimidates students or otherwise hinders learning. At the same time, instructors should continually observe their students' body language, and should use these observations to alter their presentations so that more learning will occur.

Exercises for Chapter Eight

1. What is appropriate dress for adult education instructors?

2. Prepare a list of distracting characteristics and mannerisms that instructors should avoid. How many of these have you been guilty of?

3. What can instructors do to avoid intimidating and invading students' "safe space?"

4. Prepare a list of ways in which students communicate to instructors via body language. Also, based on your experience in the classroom, suggest how instructors should interpret such body language.

End Note

[1] For a short but interesting related article, see Erichson, Earl, "What Are Those Busy Bodies Saying?" *REEAction,* Nov.-Dec. 1991, p.5

CHAPTER NINE

Audio-Visual Aids

Introduction

In Chapter Two it was noted that not all students have the same learning style. Rather, four separate learning styles were identified -- auditory, visual, tactual, and kinesthetic. Instructor knowledge of how to use audio-visual aids effectively benefits both students who learn by hearing and students who learn by seeing. Since the largest proportion of students learn visually (46 percent -- see Chapter Two), and another 22 percent learn via the auditory (aural) senses, audio-visual aids have the capacity to significantly affect the efficiency of the learning process. There is a great deal of appeal to the proposition that matching presentation aids with student learning styles should increase the efficiency of the learning process. Moreover, the learning pyramids set out in Chapter Two support this proposition.

Clearly then, an instructor's knowledge of the specific learning styles possessed by members of a given class may influence both the methods used to teach materials, as well as the selection of audio-visual aids. But particularly with continuing education classes, often there is no practical way to determine predominant student learning styles prior to the time of class preparation.

Even without specific information about student learning styles, it is reasonable to assume that the more senses used in the learning process, the greater the likelihood that more students will learn and remember. For this reason, many instructors combine the use of several audio-visual classroom aids. Audio-visual aids available include microphones, blackboards, newsprint pads/flip charts, overhead projectors, video-tape recorder/players, movie projectors, slide projectors, and slide tape combinations. Computer-based "master classrooms" also exist which make it easy to utilize multiple audio-visual aids in a single classroom presentation. Some of the major advantages and disadvantages of each audio-visual aid are briefly discussed in this chapter. A description of a master classroom (utilizing multiple audio-visual aids in a single classroom presentation) is reserved for the following chapter.

Audio Aids

Instructors with a weak voice may find it essential to use microphones in order to be heard. At the other extreme, instructors with booming voices teaching in small classrooms may never use microphones. But in longer (and larger) classes, all instructors may find microphones helpful to avoid straining and losing their voices. But for some teachers, a microphone can have a negative effect on voice quality, and may lead to a decision to not use mikes -- particularly in shorter classes and smaller classrooms.

Three basic types of microphones are available, and will be discussed in turn.

Stationary Microphones

Stationary microphones, the first type of audio aid, either stand beside or are attached to a podium or lectern. When required for hearing in a large classroom, a major disadvantage of stationary microphones is that they require instructors to remain behind the lectern. (Many regard the podium as a physical barrier between students and teachers which makes it more difficult to develop rapport with the audience.)

A second major disadvantage of stationary microphones is that they may not pick up speakers' voices well when teachers turn their heads to establish and maintain eye contact with students in various parts of the classroom. Other types of microphones, however, do not have this basic disadvantage.

Lavaliere Microphones

Lavaliere microphones, the second type of microphone, are attached to instructors' clothing via tie tacks or clips, and are connected to audio systems by cords. The portability made possible by these cords makes it easier for instructors to maintain good voice projection while moving around the room and turning their heads as audience eye contact is maintained. Obviously, longer cords permit greater movement around the room and the fact that microphones are attached to clothing keeps both hands free for both gesturing and using visual aids.

However, lavaliere microphones have at least two disadvantages. Often a heavy metal connector is used to connect these microphones (which are on short cords) to longer cords. If allowed to drag on the floor, the weight of these connectors can pull lavaliere mikes off of instructors' clothing. Thus, these connectors should be attached to instructors' belt or placed in their pockets so that the lavaliere mike is not inadvertently dislodged. Attaching connectors to belts is preferable to placing them in pockets because, on rare occasions, instructors have been shocked by electrical shorts in the connector. A personal instructor friend of the author advises that teachers should never, ever, place the connector in their front pockets!

Secondly, if instructors are not continuously aware of the location of microphone cords, it is easy to step on such cords and pull the mikes from their clothing. An even greater hazard is for instructors to get their feet tangled in the cord, trip, and make a less than graceful swan dive onto the floor. Fastening lavaliere cords to the back of instructors' belts or clothing makes entanglement and tripping less likely.

Cordless Microphones

Cordless mikes are the third basic type of microphone. Cordless microphones transmit sounds through the air to audio systems so cords are not necessary. Cordless mikes permit instructors to move around classrooms and maintain eye contact with audiences without worrying about becoming entangled in microphone cords. These mikes may be either hand-held or attached to clothing in the same manner as lavaliere mikes. Again, many instructors prefer cordless mikes to be attached to clothing to avoid arm cramps and to keep both hands available for both gesturing and working with visual aids. The audio quality of cordless mikes sometimes is not as good as with the lavaliere and stationary systems, and some cheaper remote systems may pick up unwanted and distracting radio transmissions from outside the classroom or building. To avoid a bad investment, instructors should test cordless microphone systems at the planned use site in advance of purchase. Many cordless systems are fully portable, and may be moved from classroom to classroom, as well as to different buildings and cities.

Cordless microphones often pick up and broadcast sound so long as the mikes are within 200 feet (or more) of the audio units. Thus, instructors should be sure to turn cordless microphones off during coffee and restroom breaks. Horror stories abound regarding the latter. Visualize an instructor hurrying down the hallway during a restroom break mumbling to himself or herself "I think I can make it. I think I can make it," and then "I knew I could make it!" Cordless mikes should always be turned off at break time!

Visual Aids

It already has been noted that students learn in different ways. Students making statements as simple as "I hear you!" or "I see!" provide clues as to whether such students learn important concepts by listening, or by seeing instructors write or illustrate materials on screens, blackboards, or flip charts. Clearly the use of visual aids will enhance learning for a substantial number of students. Moreover, it has been said that visual attention is roughly 25 times as great as auditory attention. Thus, the use of visual aids is important in creating an optimal learning environment. We now turn to a brief description of advantages and challenges presented by using various visual aids.

Blackboards/Greenboards

Blackboards/greenboards provide one method by which instructors can present material visually. However, material on blackboards may not be clearly visible in larger classrooms by students sitting long distances away, and chalk squeaking across blackboards may be a distraction to learning. Moreover, sometimes instructors erase materials from blackboards before all students have had time to copy them into their notes. If questions arise about materials that have already been erased, it may be necessary to take time to put the same materials on the blackboard again. Other visual aids may not require re-writing important concepts, so some argue that blackboards do not efficiently use class time. Also, chalk dust may either cause some to have difficulty breathing or to frequently sneeze, and this dust often shows on dark clothing.

However, there are two even greater disadvantages to using blackboards. First, eye contact with students is lost when instructors turn away to write on blackboards. This means that instructors temporarily lose the opportunity to use students' body language to check for comprehension of concepts being presented. (It also means they may not see and dodge articles thrown by students!)

Second, when instructors speak while facing blackboards, their voice is projecting away from students. Depending on the strength of instructors' voices, this may cause some students to have difficulty hearing.

Whiteboards

Whiteboards have many of the same advantages and disadvantages as blackboards. They differ in that using special colored markers on them may result in materials placed on the board being visible for greater distances. Special equipment or chemicals are required to clean some whiteboards, and the inadvertent use of permanent markers may make it necessary to replace the entire board.

Feltboards

Feltboards are made of cloth, and additional material (felt) may be placed on them. Sometimes called clothboards, these visual aids are seen most often in elementary classrooms. However, some instructors teaching adults use such boards effectively, as for developing graphs, and making lists of important terms (with such terms sometimes being printed on pieces of cloth).

Newsprint Pads/ Flip Charts

Newsprint pads (sometimes called flip charts) are large sheets of paper bound in tablet form and placed on tripods or other holding devices. Typically, instructors write on flip charts using broad felt tip markers of bright, contrasting colors which are visible at somewhat longer distances than chalk marks on blackboards. For this reason, flip charts often are preferred to blackboards in larger classrooms.

As with blackboards, instructors may turn away from the class when writing on newsprint pads, so both eye contact and voice projection away from classes can be problems. However, because newsprint pads are narrower than most blackboards and are placed some distance from the front wall, instructors may be able to at least partially stand beside these pads. (The same possibility exists for portable blackboards.) This permits eye contact and voice projection to be less of a problem than with stationary blackboards.

Newsprint pads are not erasable, but rather the sheets are simply "flipped over" the top of the pad after use. Thus, they can easily be flipped back over and viewed again if needed. Also, individual newsprint pad sheets may be torn off and taped around the walls for future reference. This avoids the necessity of rewriting, as where students want to view material already erased from a blackboard.

Newsprint pads have one additional advantage. They can be prepared in advance and just flipped over to introduce new materials. Alternatively, since pencil marks cannot be seen on newsprint pads from significant distances, instructors can place everything they wish to present in pencil on these pads prior to class. This makes it easy to write on these pads with markers during class without constantly referring to a separate set of teaching notes.

Overhead Projectors

Overhead projectors[1] are quite popular with adult educators. Some overheads are portable, and may be folded up into a suitcase (or other carrying case) for transporting from one place to another. Other overhead projector models cannot be folded, but typically are placed on carts for easy movement within and between classrooms in the same or nearby buildings. In either case, screens or light colored walls (see discussion in Chapter Three) are required as a projection surface when overhead projectors are used.

Instructors continuously face the class when using overhead projectors, so an advantage exists when compared to blackboards and flip charts with respect to both maintenance of eye contact and direction of voice projection. Overhead projectors require instructors to write on transparency sheets either in or before class using erasable or non-erasable pens or other techniques.

Transparencies may be prepared in advance using professional lettering devices (or software programs), and many contain illustrations and/or humorous cartoons. As a general rule, the point of cartoons should be recognizable within two to three seconds to be of maximum effectiveness. When mounted in cardboard frames for stability, transparencies may be used time after time and, in a similar manner to newsprint pads, class notes may be placed on these frames for easy reference. Access to copy machines is required to create black and white transparencies, but multi-colored transparencies also may be made through the use of color printers, photographic processes, or by the older method of cutting and pasting transparent colored materials on overhead transparency sheets. Computer software now exists by which instructors can combine clip art and color to efficiently develop truly professional transparencies.

Instructors using previously prepared transparencies should make sure that their visual aids are arranged in the proper order to avoid the appearance of disorganization when seeking the next transparency sheet. Also, transparencies already shown to the class should be kept in order so that they may quickly be retrieved and used again when answering students' questions. Keeping transparencies organized and within arm's reach is a major, important task.

Instructors need sufficient table space on which to lay their transparencies prior to and after use. Often hotels, motels and similar providers of classrooms do not provide the needed table space unless specifically requested to do so. To keep their hands free to manipulate transparencies, instructors using overhead projectors typically prefer to use microphones which attach to their clothing.

The classic mistake made with overhead transparencies is to use written or printed letters which are too small to be read by the entire class. Using a standard typewriter to prepare transparencies almost always results in print which is too small to be read. However, equipment designed to produce larger, legible lettering is readily available, and should be used by those who cannot hand letter legibly. Today, lettering often is accomplished by using computer software to develop transparency messages. A good rule of thumb is that transparency lettering is too small if a standing instructor cannot read a transparency placed on the floor.

Transparencies should contain no more than three to four major points about a specific topic. By placing a sheet of paper over the entire transparency, instructors may move the paper to successively disclose the next point when they are ready to talk about it. If these points are placed on transparencies with permanent ink, instructors may write directly on the transparencies (in the blank space between major points) with erasable ink and later erase these materials while maintaining the original transparency for future use.

Some instructors making extensive use of class discussion as a teaching technique will prepare only a few (or no) transparencies prior to class. This permits them to efficiently cover the material in whatever order is dictated by student discussion, questions and comments. Care must be taken, of course, to maintain sufficient organization and control over the direction of discussion to present materials in a logical fashion. This may require deferring answers to some questions until later.

When instructors use overhead projectors to which transparency rolls are attached, rollers are attached to both sides (or front and back) of the projectors. Each roller to which the acetate roll is attached contains a handle. Depending on the type of overhead projector, the continuous transparency sheets may be rolled either from side to side or from back to front. In either event, instructors should make sure the unused acetate rolls are placed so that they may turn the transparency rollers without reaching across projectors and casting shadows across projection surfaces. That is, if the transparency rolls from side to side, right-handed instructors should place the unused portion of the roll on the right side of machines. Similarly, left-handed instructors should place the fresh part of the roll on the left side of projectors.

When previously prepared transparencies are used in conjunction with transparency rolls, the previously prepared transparencies should be placed under the transparency rolls so that such transparency rolls may be written on without risking damage to the previously prepared transparencies. Placing transparencies in clear plastic "sleeves" for protection and organizing them in a notebook is an efficient way to use transparencies when teaching.

Some instructors prefer acetate rolls to be mounted so that they roll from back to front (rather than from side to side) causing a continuous stream of notes to appear on projection surfaces. If so, right-handed instructors should be sure that the roller handles are located on the left side of the machine. The opposite is true for left-handed instructors. Again, the location of handles should make it easy to roll the acetate without leaning across and casting shadows on the projection surface.

A disadvantage of using overhead projectors is that students wanting to see previously discussed materials must wait for the rollers to be rolled back or previously used transparencies to be retrieved and placed on projectors again. Previously covered material is not continuously available for view as are flip chart sheets taped on walls.

Sometimes instructors remove one transparency and place another on the projectors (or roll the acetate roll) without turning the machine off. This practice may be distracting, and some students report that changing transparencies in this manner actually hurts their eyes. Thus, it is recommended to turn overhead projector lights off before switching transparencies. Equipment salespeople state that turning projector lights off and on between transparency changes does not shorten the lives of projector light bulbs.

Bulbs for overhead projectors do wear out, so extra bulbs should always be available. Also, these light bulbs are expensive, so the fan should be left running to cool the bulb after turning the lights off. Failure to leave the fan running can significantly shorten bulb life.

Instructors should be careful not to block the light being projected on the screen. Likewise, they should never walk between the projector and the screen while the projector is on. Reasonable movement around the classroom not only helps to obtain and maintain student attention (as discussed in a previous chapter), but also ensures that some students view of the projection screen will not be continuously blocked.

Instructors who move away from the projector may use a battery-powered laser pointer to emphasize points shown on the screen. The disadvantage of facing the screen to use the laser pointer is that eye contact with the class temporarily is lost. For this reason, some instructors may prefer to remain near the projector and place solid arrows or projection pens on the surface to focus attention on topics being discussed. This technique can be used without facing the screen and without losing eye contact with the audience.

Instructors who move around the room while teaching can turn the overhead projector on and off by using a remote control. Remote controls are relatively inexpensive, and are a definite aid to mobile instructors.

Last but not least, overhead projectors are helpful in quickly obtaining students' attention when class begins and after refreshment breaks. Simply turning on the machines and lighting the screen is an attention getter. Turning projectors off and on again also helps regain student attention that has wandered for any reason.

Obviously, any machine can break down. Thus, instructors should always make sure overhead projectors are functioning and in proper focus before classes begin.

Some instructors report less student resistance when combining the use of an overhead projector with a flip chart, especially when asking students to "fill in the blanks" of a form being taught. Simply project the form onto the flip chart. The blanks are larger than writing on the transparency.

Today, many instructors utilize the projection of various kinds of computer-generated material using Liquid Crystal Display (LCD) panel. This typically requires a higher intensity light projection, and works best when instructors can control overhead lighting. This topic is also discussed in Chapters Ten (The Master Classroom) and Eleven (Teaching to Remote Locations).

Video Recorders/Players

The classroom use of videotape recorders/players is of relatively recent origin. When classes extend over several periods, each session may be videotaped and made available to students who missed one or more classes. This procedure works particularly well for classes at which attendance is mandatory, as it may avoid the necessity for students to sit through the entire course again when a session is missed because of personal emergencies. The obvious disadvantage of this procedure is that students do not have the opportunity to ask questions when viewing a video tape. For this reason, instructors who videotape their lectures for viewing later need to set aside time for students to obtain answers to such questions. Two-way communication is essential for optimal learning.

Allowing students to view, at their leisure, tapes of math and financing classes has been popular in at least one school. Students report that they can "freeze" the instructor, take their time while working the problem, and then replay the concept if it went by too quickly.

Many instructors use videotape players in an entirely different fashion. Professionally prepared videotapes are available for classroom use on a number of topics. Such professionally prepared videotapes work most efficiently when followed by discussion periods in which students may ask questions to qualified instructors. This is referred to as "video-enhanced instruction." Failing to provide the opportunity for discussion and questions following videotape presentations often results in lower than desired levels of learning, because under these circumstances only one-way communication is possible.

Also, videotape players must either have large screens, or several monitors must be scattered at strategic points throughout large classrooms if the videotape is to be seen and heard by all. For this reason, as well as equipment cost, video-tape players are used most often in relatively small classes and classrooms. It goes without saying, of course, that people must be present in the classroom (usually instructors) who know how to run the equipment and be "trouble-shooters" when mechanical problems arise.

Movie Projectors

Movie projectors are similar to videotape players with respect to their advantages and disadvantages. Professionally prepared movies on specific topics can be good teaching tools, particularly when followed by discussion periods. All students must be able to see projection surfaces and hear sound tracks, and the special projection equipment required may be both expensive and unavailable in some teaching locations. Also, both knowledge of how to run the equipment and trouble-shooting ability is essential for optimal results.

Often the classroom lights must be dimmed or turned off when showing movies. Turning lights off or down may make it difficult for students to take notes as well as making some sleepy.

Perhaps the ideal physical classroom layout for showing movies is the rear projection room described in the next chapter.

Slide Projectors

A few instructors make extensive use of slide projectors and previously prepared trays of 2 x 2 slides. They use remote controls, of course, to successively display new slides. Instructors may more or less continuously face the audience while showing slides, thereby maintaining eye contact and achieving good voice projection.

Slides may be used in a similar fashion to overhead transparencies. That is, if three major points are to be made under a given topic, the major point may be shown with the first slide, the second slide can then show the first and second point (while highlighting the second), and so forth.

Professional preparation of slides can be expensive. Less expense is involved when instructors or other staff members have artistic flairs. Colored illustrations may be prepared in convenient sizes, and pictures of these illustrations taken with slide film. Once developed, these slides are placed in order in slide trays and the slide presentation is ready. Changes in presentations may be made by inserting additional new slides.

Deviating from the planned order of presentation and placing previously covered material on the screen again is less efficient when using slides than with transparencies. This is because the remote control will briefly show each slide between the current and desired one as instructors search for a particular slide. Thus, those heavily using class discussion may find slides somewhat less efficient than other visual aids.

Instructors must keep a supply of projector light bulbs available, and be adept at trouble-shooting mechanical problems that arise. Also, irrespective of whether or not professional preparation is utilized, costs for slide preparation typically are somewhat higher than for many other audio-visual aids. Some instructors have felt that developing technology was making the use of 2 x 2 slides somewhat obsolete. However, computers are bringing slides back, so slides may work well with computer-assisted instruction (particularly for large audiences).

Slide/Tape Combinations

Some instructors may utilize from one to five slide projectors on a large projection surface, with the entire audio presentation on tape. Recorded background music may further professionalize the slide/tape presentation. This may be prohibitively expensive for many instructors, as professional assistance is often required to prepare and coordinate slide/tape presentations. Again, following slide/tape presentations with the opportunity for class interaction and discussion may be essential for two-way communication and optimal learning.

Because of cost, developing technology, and other factors, many believe that the availability of videotapes has made the use of slide/tape combination obsolete.

Summary

Choices of audio-visual aids may be affected by classroom size, cost, availability of equipment, the type of teaching technique employed, and the particular topic being taught. The important point to keep in mind is that the use of audio-visual aids can result in increasing the amount of classroom learning -- particularly for visual and auditory learners.

Exercises for Chapter Nine

1. List the advantages and disadvantages of using each of the three basic types of microphones.

2. Plan and prepare classroom presentations using at least three different types of visual aids. Compare these with currently used visual aids. Can instructors become more effective by using new and different audio-visual aids?

End Note

[1] For an excellent article on this topic, see Wilcox, Sherry and Chuck Wilcox, *REEAction*, Fall, 1989, pp. 6-7.

CHAPTER TEN

The Master Classroom

Introduction

The technologically focused teaching aids available to teachers have moved far beyond the black (white) board and overhead projector found in traditional classrooms. Classrooms are being equipped with increasingly sophisticated teaching equipment, and frequently this equipment is being/can be used to teach classes at remote locations.

With this in mind, the purpose of this chapter is threefold. The first objective is to describe the tools which instructors have available in "master classrooms." These master classrooms are typical of those found on many college campuses and also in some proprietary schools. The second objective is to identify some advantages and challenges to instructors created by the master classroom environment. A discussion of the advantages and challenges of using master classroom technology to teach audiences at remote locations is reserved for Chapter Eleven.

Master Classroom Capabilities[1]

The capabilities of master classrooms include:

1. CD-ROM;
2. cable television;
3. closed circuit television;
4. VHS/VCR playback;
5. overhead visual presenters for hard copy;
6. external audio/visual inputs;

7. video disc with barcode scanner;
8. external capability to synchronize colors;
9. remote control slide projector access;
10. microphone built into house audio system;
11. both IBM and Macintosh based software applications;
12. wireless audio link system for the hearing impaired; and
13. full projection capability for all video sources.

The master classroom instructor has much greater control over both light and sound than exists in the typical classroom. Experts working with and designing mediated lecture space believe that it is this control over light and sound which leads to a more dynamic communication and learning experience. Control over light and sound comes from the diverse set of equipment required to facilitate the master classroom capabilities previously set out. Equipment costs may be higher when added to existing classrooms than when installed at the time of construction (about $30,000 as this is written in 1995). On the other hand, depending on the talents of the individual instructor, the topic being taught, and the specific technology needed, only a portion of the equipment might be required to upgrade a specific classroom.

Although technologically-improved equipment costs have been decreasing over time, newly designed "bells and whistles" likely will continue to be available for a long time to come. While equipment costs will always be a central concern for business decision-makers, such costs need not be prohibitive and may well lead to a more efficient learning process.

Design Features

Professionals designing mediated lecture space (i.e., master classrooms) have many concerns similar to those discussed in REEA's Instructor Development Workshop (IDW) and in this textbook. Of particular relevance are the physical aspects of the classroom and audio-visual equipment. A brief overview of the physical features of a master classroom follows.

Room Design

Mediated lecture space designers prefer rooms that are long and narrow rather than wide and shallow. This long narrow arrangement is perceived to improve the overall screen viewing quality from all seats in the room. Projections viewed from side angles appear less bright. The mediated lecture space designers argue, of course, that students will learn less if the material on the screen is not clear to them. This principle is particularly important to visual learners.

A control room is located at the back of the classroom. A technician located there may assist with showing 16 mm or 35 mm films, as well as controlling both sound and lighting. The teaching station (podium, which can be locked between classes) is located to the side of the projection service so that it is out of students' line of sight to the projection screen. Light, sound and all multi-media equipment also can be controlled from the teaching station.

If ceilings are 10 feet or more high, ceiling-mounted video projectors are used to avoid interfering with films shown from the rear projection booth.

Numerous electrical outlets are found in walls, floor, and ceilings. For safety, their locations are outside of normal traffic patterns. Conduits for wiring also are interspersed through the ceiling, walls, and floor. Storage is provided near the front of the room for any portable audio-visual material which the instructor may choose to use.

Tiered seating is used to make it easier to see the screen and instructor. Access ramps are sloped gently for handicapped accessibility.

Lighting

Separate banks of florescent lights permit some lighting to be dimmed or turned off when movie projectors are utilized. Separately controlled incandescent lights are located above the students to provide pools of light for note-taking.

Lighting controls are located near the entrance door, at the instructor teaching station, and in the rear projection room. Blinds and/or blackout drapes are on all windows to facilitate viewing of projections.

Sound

Master classroom floors are carpeted to reduce noise. Wireless microphones permit teachers to move about freely. Multiple microphone jacks are located at the front (for use by panels of experts) and in the aisles (so that students asking questions may be heard). The volume, tone, and equalization of all microphones can be controlled both at the teaching station and in the rear projection room. FM receivers are available throughout the room for those with hearing problems.

Two sound systems are present. The "public address" system has speakers mounted in the ceiling. A theater quality sound system has speakers on each side of the projection surface, and is used for audio and/or video tapes.

Projection Screen

The projection screen has a white matte finish to brighten projections. The recommended screen size is one inch of width for each seat in the classroom. The bottom of the screen is four feet off the floor so that those sitting in the back of the room can view the entire screen.

The (motorized) screens may be angled at a push of a button to accommodate different kinds of projections. A single location screen angled to make the bottom and top portion of an overhead projector surface equally readable would cause a portion of the picture from a ceiling mounted video projector to be out of focus. For this reason a second screen is placed near the front of the stage area to focus a second visual aid when two visual aids are used at the same time. Motorized retractable screens are preferred (though more expensive) because the screens are less susceptible to damage than pull-down screens.

Interconnections

Other connections available to facilitate instruction include telephone, access to cable television, access to the mainframe computer, and access to other area or local computer networks. The latter may permit an instructor to access materials, such as stored transparency figures, from the instructor's personal computer located in his or her office.

These interconnections also permit video to be played back, and personal (e.g., laptop) computers to be utilized. Other multi-media interconnections available (either hard-wired or wireless) include those for a CD-ROM player, video disc player, and an audio cassette player/recorder.

Advantages and Challenges of the Master Classroom

Physical Layout and Equipment

Advantages. The master classroom physical arrangement facilitates eye contact, voice projection, and good screen clarity for the student viewers seated throughout the room. The podium allows the instructor continuously to face the audience while operating the equipment. The design achieves a very good, perhaps even optimal, utilization of the technical features of the various multi-media equipment.

Challenges. Master classroom design features seem to emphasize maximizing available technological capabilities to aid instructors' (particularly lecturers') "performance" efforts. However, videotaping capabilities have not been routinely incorporated in master classroom design. In some courses, videotaping has been used effectively to achieve instruction improvement via teacher self-assessment and invited or imposed peer reviews. Videotaping also may be used to provide students the opportunity to view missed class sessions, although such viewing is not a perfect substitute for attending class because it does not ensure two-way communication.

Technology and design choices associated with the master classroom seem to anticipate the lecture mode of instruction, perhaps to the exclusion of other, more participative, learning approaches. Highly effective instructors seek and achieve enhanced two-way communication between themselves and their students in classroom settings. Some master classroom design features may interfere with these well proven and (often) preferred participative approaches. The podium setup restricts the instructor's movements; however, some (but not all) media have remote control capabilities. The tiered classroom makes it physically difficult to involve students in "task" or "break-out" groups, although it can be done by using two rows (with a recorder/reporter in the front row). Many instructors using task groups prefer seating configuration of tables, each accommodating two to six students, arranged for easy instructor access.

Some physical modifications may enhance the master classroom's capability to accommodate both lecture and more participative (active) methods of instruction. Alternatively, though probably less desirable (from the standpoint of cost), two distinct physical designs (each geared to the appropriate anticipated instruction method) may be warranted.

The technical aspects of equipment present another set of challenges. The added complexity of master classroom features makes familiarization with full equipment capabilities difficult. The average instructor initially will be unfamiliar even with sound and light capabilities. Informal and ad-hoc training can prove ineffective for meeting these challenges. Inevitable operational problems and technical equipment glitches also necessitate a "back-up" procedure, such as a support technician's on-call telephone advice. Stickers with (technician) emergency numbers may be mounted on the telephones located at the podium to ensure that instructors have immediate access to support technicians.

Last but not least, the long narrow classroom is at odds with conventional wisdom that it is easier for instructors to develop and maintain rapport with students who are physically closer. Also, reasonable instructor movement may be possible in the master classroom only when a technician is present (at the back of the classroom) to operate the equipment as needed.

Logical Design Features

Advantages. The master classroom offers the instructor a variety of presentation formats, including videotape, video disc, computer graphics, and transparency and hard-copy (visual) projections (e.g., directly from a printed page). Windows software allows more than one open window. Thus, an instructor could display output from the computer related to real property valuations, interrupt and show a portion of a videotape of a real estate development project, pause and project a hard-copy of the latest *Wall Street Journal* column related to valuing real estate, and return to the computer to continue the "normal" presentation.

Visual learning assists many students with information retention. Instructors have access to equipment that offers them a vast array of ways to enhance their visual presentations. The instructor's before- class preparation benefits from a high level of focus and organization in the same manner that preparation benefits learning in less technologically sophisticated classrooms. However, aided by the technology, the instructor has the opportunity to demonstrate the effectiveness of formulating visual aids depicting both "non-technical" overviews and "technical" details. Computer-aided graphics facilitate planning and organization of materials. Standardized formats that use titles, headings and sub-headings encourage instructors to identify and focus on both primary and secondary presentation objectives. These formats can be used to synthesize material and limit it to only what is necessary for a specific learning purpose. Graphic software includes standard ways to sort, view and re-sort the order of visual presentation materials. The capabilities of viewing a slide show and/or obtaining hard copy printouts of pages with 4-6 slides per page can help the instructor see teaching materials from the audience's perspective. Continuous instructional improvement directions can be identified and achieved if time is taken to self-criticize and self-evaluate the teaching materials. Computerization provides a myriad of opportunities to save and document teaching materials for future comparison and referral.

Computer-aided graphics offer readability, variety and interest to the learner. Standard readable type sizes are preprogrammed into "master" formats. For example in Figure 10-1, Chart A was redesigned as Chart B by simply pointing and clicking. Graphic formats feature many colors, font and graphic styles. Clip art illustrations do not need to be detailed to be effective and the preprogrammed options provide pictures suitable for many purposes. Software packages make the creative use of color available. This is important, because the effective use of color has been shown to aid memory retention.

Step-by-step demonstrations, such as how to access a computerized multiple listing service, can be taught more efficiently because all students can view monitors (shown on the screen) simultaneously. Also, computerized development and display facilitates partitioning slides into digestible and manageable parts. For example, a building's entire floor plan can be drawn on one slide. By making copies after each successive deletion and rearranging the slides, the presenter can depict the drawing of the floor plan from the exterior dimensions to each room's interior dimensions in a step-by-step manner. Students can be asked to visualize the next step before they see it on the screen. Successive transparencies can accomplish the same outcome, but costs tend to cause the instructor to limit the number of transparencies used (particularly when the instructor must prepare and bear the expense of multiple copies).

Using the computer terminal to record notes from class discussion may provide more readable "flip chart" documentation. Items can be rearranged easily or duplicated and modified. In other words, computer software access adds a whole new dimension to composing and documenting class discussion for subsequent use as classroom aids. Similarly, on-screen open-ended participation questions can be offered to the entire class and, after allowing time for group discussion, on-screen note-taking can begin.

Challenges. A major challenge for the master classroom concerns the required level of instructor motivation to design and develop materials that make the system effective. (Prepackaged instructional aids for the master classroom are still scarce.) Simply learning to use equipment involves a sizable time commitment. Learning to *fully utilize* equipment requires even more dedication and commitment.

Keeping materials organized and accessible is important. Master classroom equipment can introduce a degree of rigidity to any presentation sequence. Changing the presentation sequence and maintaining flexibility and adaptability during class presents new challenges. Instructors need training and familiarization with options afforded by the equipment. Perhaps overcoming these challenges is analogous to learning an art rather than a science.

Before perceived and actual problems can be solved, such problems and their feasible solutions must be identified. For example, some instructors formulate "flip chart" pages and tape or tack them around the room. The single screen format of the master classroom may require some creative sizing and pasting of the screen layout to achieve the same learning outcome.

As in any classroom environment, the instructor seeks to gauge and adapt to students' understanding of the knowledge or skill area, and then either provide more in-depth information or proceed to the next point. The challenge is to NOT allow the equipment to dictate the content, but rather to insist that learners' needs pace and guide the learning process. In other words, being prepared means having (but not necessarily presenting) a branch of the learning tree to respond to the question, "Who needs more detail about this area?" Obviously, this approach means that some

Figure 10-1: An Example of Master Formats

Limitations to Ownership Rights

- Public
  - Police Power
  - Eminent Domain
  - Taxation
  - Escheat
- Private
  - Liens
  - Easements
  - Restrictive Covenants

Chart A

Limitations to Ownership Rights

- *Public*
  - *Police Power*
  - *Eminent Domain*
  - *Taxation*
  - *Escheat*
- *Private*
  - *Liens*
  - *Easements*
  - *Restrictive Covenants*

Chart B

impressive presentation materials will not be shown to every class, notwithstanding their required preparation time.

Similarly, instructors would be wise to avoid the temptation to rely exclusively on the screen and omit analogies, personal stories, examples, etc. The proven effectiveness of interesting and relevant real world examples warrants their inclusion in the learning process. Do not neglect to use understandable (preplanned or ad hoc) analogies that make the unfamiliar familiar.

Finally, an attempt to always use all equipment may be inappropriate to learning goals. Currently the content and quality of video productions about real estate concepts does not illustrate the linkage of scenes on the videotape with underlying concepts. Thus, guidance for class time allocations that seek to play videotapes X percent of the time are inappropriate.

Summary

The term "master classroom" is used to describe a classroom which features technologically state-of-the-art audio-visual aids. Many master classrooms were designed to facilitate teaching using the lecture technique, so the physical layout often provides instructors with real challenges when they want to employ interactive learning techniques. In a final analysis, teaching techniques requiring class interaction can be employed effectively in master classrooms. Care must be taken to remember that the master classroom technology is a tool to facilitate learning, and such technology should not be regarded as an end in and of itself.

Technology is opening new vistas of opportunities for instructors. These technological opportunities provide instructors with both advantages and challenges. The technological frontier is dynamic, and will provide more advantages than challenges. Training professionals who either ignore or are complacent about this dynamic technological teaching frontier risk falling behind and becoming the dinosaur of the twenty-first century. Teachers using master classrooms may be required to alter their traditional classroom teaching techniques (but hopefully only slightly) if optimal learning is to occur in mediated classrooms.

The cost of furnishing classrooms with multi-media equipment is significant and tends to limit the use of the master classrooms to larger class sizes. However, multi-media technological innovations are lowering costs to the point that much required hardware and software is becoming affordable.

Exercises for Chapter Ten

1. Visit a master classroom and make a list of the technology-related audio-visual teaching aids. For a section within one of the classes which you teach, develop a plan for utilizing master classroom technology on a topic which you consider to be one of your weakest. Be sure to include plans for teaching part of this topic using interactive techniques. Will master classroom technology improve your presentation and increase student learning?

2. Repeat the first exercise, but this time develop a plan for using master classroom technology on a topic which you believe to be one of your strongest.

Figures

Figure 10-1: An Example of Master Formats.

End Note

[1] This chapter is based on Christensen, Linda, and Don Levi, DREI, "The Master Classroom at Wichita State University," *Journal of the Real Estate Educators Association*, pp. 7-12, June, 1995.

CHAPTER ELEVEN

Teaching to Remote Locations

Introduction

Make no mistake, teaching to remote locations is significantly different than teaching to purely on-site audiences. To achieve the best possible performance, even hand, arm, and body movements need to be considered while the teacher remains in camera range at all times. To illustrate the former, in at least one remote location delivery system (compressed television), arm and hand movements often are blurred so making only minimal hand and body movements are less distracting to students.

If the typical live classroom is thought of as an on-stage performance, such on-stage performance efforts must be "juiced up" a few notches when presentations are broadcast to remote locations. Even if one's first remote location presentation is planned and prepared for like never before, instructors still are likely to discover a number of things which can be changed to make a second remote location presentation more effective. In this section different levels of remote location educational delivery systems are described. This is followed by a list of suggested "How To's" for instructors who have little or no remote location teaching experience.

Identifying Remote Location Educational Delivery Systems

Currently there are three distinct levels of delivering educational programs to remote locations. (Remote locations may include the next room, the next building, or a classroom in a town a thousand miles away.) At the lowest level, an open telephone line may constitute the sole method of communication. Two-way communication is possible, and could be initiated by student question/comments or by an instructor's use of class discussion. Since the instructor cannot see the students (and vice versa), body language cannot be used to check for comprehension. The lack of eye contact makes it more difficult to develop rapport with students, and those who learn visually may learn less than they would in on-site (and other kinds of remote) classrooms. Clearly a scheme for timely distribution of written materials is essential if visual learners are to be able to learn efficiently under this type of educational delivery system.

The second level of educational delivery to remote locations involves televising the instructor's presentation to remote locations, and providing an open telephone line from remote classrooms to the instructor at his/her central location. (This delivery system is referred to as "Talkback Television" in some areas.) Relatively better two-way communication is possible under this scenario (as compared to the open phone line being the exclusive method of communicating), and the efficiency of the learning process may be improved somewhat for visual learners. The fact that the instructor does not have eye contact with students may cause special efforts to be expended to develop an "acceptable" level of rapport with the class. Moreover, visual checks of body language are not possible, so instructors need to develop alternative ways of checking for comprehension and determining when it is time to move on to the next topic. This scenario seems to work best when a live class is being televised -- perhaps in part because students in live classrooms often have the same questions as those in remote locations.

The final remote location educational delivery system might best be described as "interactive television". This delivery system not only provides a televised view of the instructor to remote location(s), but also includes monitors permitting instructors to simultaneously view each and every remote classroom. It is the method that requires the least alteration of instructors' standard on-site teaching techniques, but even still significant changes in style and teaching techniques will improve the teaching performance. Students at remote locations may direct questions to the instructor verbally, or by either fax or e-mail.

Some education providers video-tape presentations made under one of the last two remote location delivery systems discussed, and make such videotapes the principle teaching aid for classes held later. If optimal learning is to occur when students view these videotapes, it is critically important that experts be available to discuss the tape and answer student questions. Any educational delivery system is sub-optimal if it does not permit (and encourage) two-way communication.

Some Suggested "How To's" for Teaching to Remote Locations[1]

The following section assumes televising is the medium used to teach remote locations. For this reason, the following comments are applicable to any televised presentation.

Talk to the Site Technician

Contact the presentation site technician far in advance (at least thirty days). Ask questions about the size of the presentation room, the number and locations of cameras to be used, and the configuration of the area from which one is presenting (permanent desk? raised platform?).

Give your Outline to the Site Technician

It is good to time your outline, marking both breaks, and insertion points for overheads and other handout materials (e.g., using OH and HO as symbols). The instructor must decide what cues will be used to communicate with the technician, and whether or not a 3-minute alert before breaks and/or the end of the presentation is desired. (When using satellite and the scheduled time elapses, the program is finished with no time for good-byes!)

How Will Student Questions be Handled?

Make sure it is understood exactly how students will be asking questions (verbally, via fax or e-mail). How has the technician seen questions handled most effectively in other presentations from this studio? It may be best to block-out designated periods of time to handle questions (i.e., before or after a break). Handling fax and e-mail questions after breaks may be most efficient from students' perspectives (but may leave no break-time for the instructor).

Understand the Overhead and Audio-visual Capabilities

Be sure to spend time with the site technician (again, far in advance) discussing how overhead and other audio-visual systems operate. Do not assume that the same overheads used for on-site presentations will work well when beamed to remote locations -- each medium and site can be radically different!

Types of Overhead Systems

The ones the author(s) has(have) encountered are: (1) a "lipstick" (small overhead visual presenter) camera pointing down from the ceiling that shoots an exact *paper* copy (horizontally) of what is laid on the presentation table mark (no transparencies allowed); (2) a separate large camera that shoots an exact duplicate (including transparencies) of what is placed on the presentation table; and (3) a studio that had no capability to shoot overheads from the presentation area, so upon signal from the instructor the technician had to computer-generate anew each overhead. (Note: Overhead projectors are not conducive to camera environments since they project too much light and projections are tough to photograph.)

Designing Overheads

The overheads used should be simplistic with large-size print. Color overheads are especially effective (the MTV approach), and simple graphics are great. As with all overheads, less is more!

Site Monitors

It is essential that a person be present to serve as a monitor at each site. On-site monitors serve as a liaison to the instructor, handle problems, pass out forms/materials, and transmit questions to the presenter (especially when written and sent by fax or e-mail.)

Acknowledge Each Site

Acknowledge each site separately at the beginning of your presentation. This builds rapport and also lets the other sites know exactly where everyone is. It helps to introduce each site monitor, too, as they might not have had time to introduce themselves before the broadcast began.

The First Questions are the Toughest!

Do not be surprised if no one responds the first time questions are requested. The remote location medium is new to students, so in lieu of seeking questions, instructors may ask a site for feedback on the material so far. That way no one is embarrassed, but two-way communication is achieved and the ice is broken.

"Pregnant" Pauses

Be sure to pause after asking questions to allow students to reply from distant sites. Some systems require three to five-second delays before the question is heard, and require the same amount of time for a response to return. Many instructors find it difficult to adjust to this delay.

Set the Ground Rules for Student Questions

If fax or e-mail is used for students' questions, make sure this is mentioned early and that students are encouraged not to wait until the last 15 minutes of the presentation to send their questions. If all questions are sent at the end, often it is not possible to cover them all, and with this medium it is not possible for students to walk up after class to get their question answered.

Move Slowly, Fluidly

Keep body movements somewhat slow and deliberate. Depending on transmission quality, sudden movements may come out distorted and surreal (this is particularly true for compressed television).

A Break Time Clock

A time clock counting down on the screen is great at breaks to see time elapsed and get students back in their seats in a timely manner. It's amazing how well it works! (Ask the technician if a clock is available.)

Timing the Presentation

The time it takes to present material actually *lengthens* in this medium (possibly because of the theatrics being employed). Answering questions can take up to 25 percent longer than usual (actual questions often need to be paraphrased and clarified before answering).

Over and Out!

If possible, sign out with each site. Thank them for their participation and give them some "one-on-one" attention. Be sure to thank the monitors, and remind them to gather evaluations, continuing education forms, and other materials.

Watch Those Clothes!

Vibrant colors suitable for on-site classrooms do not work as well on television. Stay away from reds (which tend to bleed and expand somewhat) and all-white outfits (Casper the Ghost!). Solid dark colors work best. Dark-colored paisleys or small patterns for blouses, scarves and ties are okay -- but in moderation. (Has Connie Chung ever been seen on camera in Hawaiian prints?)

The Angle is Everything!

The instructor should be positioned so that the camera is somewhat above him/her, shooting down. An upward camera angle is more likely to capture such things as double chins and puffy eyes. (Yes, it's true that cameras do add about 10-15 pounds that most do not need!)

To Script or Not to Script?

If speaking from a prepared script, the instructor should work with it until he/she does not have to constantly look down. (The camera is sure to focus on down-cast eyes.) If a TelePrompTer is to be used part of the time, it is good to have at least the introductory and exit words memorized so that the instructor can be more natural and have greater freedom of physical movement if needed (like entering and exiting).

Write It Like Instructors Say It!

When writing the presentation, it does not matter how great it looks on paper. The key is, how does it *sound*? Is it casual, like the way an instructor would talk to someone one-on-

one? (Additionally, it will be much tougher to memorize if it does not flow naturally.)

Timing the Presentation

The medium of television absorbs a massive amount of words -- so what took two hours to write, might take only two minutes to deliver! Try not to be just a "talking head". Integrate computer-generated slides and "show and tell" objects into the presentation to vary the pace.

Voice-Overs (the Key to Flexibility)

It is interesting to note that television reporters covering a story are not always on camera. This is because film footage was shot first and the voice-over commentary added later in the studio. By using this same technique, this gives presenters the benefit of a scripted presentation without the hassle of having to memorize it and/or use a TelePrompTer. This approach is great when using bullet points on slides to summarize material, and especially good for technical material that needs visual adaptation.

Last But Not Least

Have fun! Do not let the new medium dictate a teaching style that is significantly different than what has worked well in the past. At the same time, do not be afraid to try new approaches when they appear warranted.

Course Approval Considerations

Pre-license, post-license, and mandatory continuing education course providers face different regulatory approval regulations in different states. Moreover, concerns about ensuring the quality and integrity of courses beamed to remote locations led the Association of Real Estate License Law Official (ARELLO) to develop and adopt a "white paper" in 1995 describing how distance education technology could result in a quality educational experience.

Entitled "Considerations in Approving Distance Education," the white paper discusses interaction with students, the overall learning environment, and course design, as well as considerations bearing on the course approval decision which involve both instructors and support services. Readers can order a copy by purchasing the *1996 ARELLO Digest*. The address is:

> ARELLO
> P.O. Box 129
> Centerville, UT 84014-0129
> Phone 801-298-5572.

Summary

This chapter builds on the previous chapter which described technology available in master classrooms by suggesting some ideas to consider when teaching classes in which at least some students are viewing the presentation from off-site locations. Teaching to remote locations may involve delivery techniques ranging from open telephone lines to interactive television.

Teaching to remote locations is an entirely new "ball game" for many instructors, and optimal learning often requires instructors to modify their teaching style and presentation techniques. But, at the same time, instructors should be encouraged to retain what traditionally has worked well for them.

An interesting but currently unanswered question for researchers is whether or not overall learning and retention is greater in master than in traditional classrooms, and whether or not learning in remote locations matches that associated with on-site teaching. Hopefully, answers to these questions will be forthcoming in the near future.

Exercise for Chapter Eleven

1. Visit a studio/classroom from which presentations are broadcast to remote locations. Then make a detailed list of changes needed in your favorite class if and when it is taught for remote locations.

End Note

[1] Julie Garton-Good, DREI, is primarily responsible for many of the "How To" ideas found later. With her permission, this section borrows from "Is the Camera On Yet?-- Mastering TV, Video, and Teleconference Presentations" which she presented to the 1995 REEA Annual Conference.

CHAPTER TWELVE

Preparing Exams and Examination Questions

Introduction

Examination performance is one method by which instructors gauge how much and how well students learn. However, it should also be recognized that, if graded and returned promptly, examinations can also be effective teaching (learning) devices. But if exams are not graded and returned for several days or weeks, students forget why they answered questions in particular ways, so the usefulness of examinations as teaching tools may be lost.

In general, the type and content of examination questions varies, depending on the course subject, level, and learning objectives. For lower level learning objectives, questions requiring information recall are appropriate. But for some higher (cognitive) levels of course objectives, exams should do more than test the ability to recall information. Rather, at these levels exams should test abilities to analyze factual situations and solve practical and relevant problems.

An Overview of Preparing Examinations

Preparing Good Exams

Preparing good exams/examination questions may well be the most difficult part of teaching. Care must be taken not to include questions that are open to more than one interpretation. Likewise, instructors must make sure that all required information is provided so that each question may be answered properly. If at all possible, instructors should take preliminary drafts of exams themselves (or ask other knowledgeable people to take preliminary exam drafts) in order to eliminate "bad" questions, and to make sure the exam is free of typographical and other errors.

In spite of instructors' best efforts, occasionally "bad" questions are included on examinations. If so, instructors must decide how to grade these questions and still be fair. If two alternative logical interpretations exist, often it is best to give full credit for all logical answers. Instructors who only give credit for the interpretation which they intended may be viewed as inflexible, and their credibility with students may be lost or seriously damaged. Clearly, maintaining credibility with students is important in fostering an optimal learning environment.

The scope of examination questions should be determined by the range of instruction required. Instructors wishing to write practical questions might use a simple checklist, such as:

1. Does the question check job-related knowledge, ability, or skills?

2. Is this knowledge, ability, or skill worthwhile to possess?

3. Is the knowledge, ability, or skill something that students should bring to the job or acquire on the job?

Length of Exams

Some students work quickly through exams; others do not. On essay questions, some students write faster than others. If exams are to evaluate how much learning is occurring, it is important that exams not be so long that they simply become "speed" tests.

Obviously, those preparing exams know both what questions are on the exam and the correct answers. Thus, one prospective measure of the length of examinations is how long it takes the instructor to personally answer all questions. Depending on both the types of questions and individual instructors, the rule of thumb has arisen that instructors should be able to prepare the key to the exams in one-third to one-half the time available to students.

Another "after the fact" rule of thumb is available to judge the appropriateness of the length of exams. Tests are about the right length when the first student finishes in one-half the allotted time.

Open book tests generally are longer and more difficult than closed book exams. At the same time, some instructors use open book exams in an attempt to overcome adult students' anxieties about test taking.

Types of Questions

Identifying Alternative Kinds of Questions

Several different kinds of questions may be asked on examinations, including true-false, multiple choice, definitions, matching, fill-in-the-blanks, listing, mathematical problems, short answers, and full-blown essay questions. Some students complain that they have interpretation problems and do not perform well on at least one of these types of questions. In fact, some students make this complaint about all available types of questions. Whether this is true is subject to conjecture, because top students often score high, irrespective of the types of questions employed. But even so, in deference to students who dislike particular types of questions, some instructors use a few of each type question on the theory that "spreading out the misery" is fairer to all concerned.

True-False Questions

Most true-false questions are a relatively short statement which students are asked to mark either true or false. Students may be asked to respond to each question by:

1. placing a T or F in a blank provided for each question;

2. writing the word true or false in the blank provided;

3. circling the correct response (T or F, True or False);

4. striking the incorrect response (T or F, True or False); or

5. when machine scoring is used, blackening the T or F in the appropriate column, circle, or box.

Arguments about scoring may subsequently arise if option number one is used. Some students can be quite creative in making the letters T and F look deceptively similar.

Option number four also should probably be avoided, as striking the incorrect answer may be confusing and cause some students to miss questions to which they know the answer. The third option, circling the correct response, may be preferable because it avoids handwriting interpretation problems and is simple to grade.

Most true-false questions simply ask students to recall information. True-false questions often must be several sentences long before they can effectively determine whether students can apply principles taught to important and practical problems. Thus, if instructors want to determine whether students understand the practical application of important principles, other types of questions sometimes may work better.

It is difficult to prepare good true-false questions that accurately discriminate regarding different levels of student knowledge. The words "always", "never", and similar terms tip off answers to adept test-takers. Obviously, wording which tips off the answer should be avoided.

Some instructors use modified true-false questions. These instructors may require students to explain *why* a question is false. To receive credit for a false answer, the student must both select false as the choice and give the correct explanation. Modified true-false questions take more time to score, but do help lessen the chance that students will score well by guessing. Otherwise, it may be possible for students to score 50 percent by simply flipping a coin for each question. To this extent, true-false questions do not always accurately discriminate among levels of student knowledge.

Another disadvantage to true-false questions is that some students tend to remember previously administered true-false questions better than they remember the answers. If they have seen the same question before, some tend to remember it as true. For this reason, it is possible that the use of true-false questions may result in students completing a class and going away with some bad information.

Multiple Choice Questions

Students sometimes refer to multiple choice questions as "multiple guess." This suggests that guessing the correct answer is possible, so multiple choice questions may be similar to true-false questions in that they do not always accurately discriminate among levels of knowledge.

There are at least three varieties of multiple choice questions. All consist of the use of a "stem," with several choices being offered to complete an accurate response. The correct choice is referred to as the "key," and incorrect choices are "distracters." In general, the stem should contain all verbiage except that which is essential to the choice (key). To illustrate an incorrect stem, consider the following question:

1. A right of survivorship:

   A. is associated with a tenancy in common

   B. is associated with a joint tenancy

   C. is associated with a corporation

   D. is associated with a partnership

A better way to write this question would be:

1. A right of survivorship is associated with a:

   A. tenancy in common

   B. joint tenancy

   C. corporation

   D. partnership

Most multiple choice questions are constructed in this manner, with only one correct choice present. Offering illogical choices should be avoided, as this permits adept test-takers to quickly eliminate wrong answers and arrive at the correct answer via the process of elimination. As a result, illogical answers make it possible to achieve high scores through guessing rather than through knowledge.

Some instructors have a tendency to place a more than proportionate number of correct choices in the same location. C is the choice most often used. Their apparent logic is that they want to force the student to evaluate all choices, so they begin with A and B as incorrect choices, place the correct choice at C, and then add a fourth (perhaps illogical) choice as D.

Making a particular choice the correct answer in a disproportionate fashion needs to be avoided, as does making the correct choice consistently longer (or shorter) than the distracters. Some students figure out such patterns quickly, and score well by guessing the predominant correct choice on questions to which they do not know the answer.

A second type of multiple choice question (called a two-stem question) is illustrated as follows:

1. A right of survivorship is associated with a

   I. joint tenancy

   II. tenancy by entireties

   A. I only is true

   B. II only is true

   C. Both I and II are true

   D. Neither I nor II is true

To answer this type of multiple choice question correctly, it is necessary to know two bits of information. And it is for this very reason that two-stem multiple choice questions may not accurately reveal the relative extent of different students' knowledge.

To illustrate, suppose two students do not know 10 (different) bits of information required to make a perfect score. Depending on how these unknown bits of information are combined in the two-stem multiple choice questions, it is possible for one of these students to miss only five questions (i.e., two bits of unknown information per question) while the other student misses ten questions (i.e., one bit of information per question). Thus, it can be argued that this type of multiple choice question inherently is an inaccurate gauge of knowledge.

The third basic type of multiple choice question might best be referred to as multiple-multiple choice. Multiple-multiple choice questions can be constructed more quickly than standard multiple choice questions (which is a plus in the minds of some instructors), and permit more than one correct answer for each question. For example:

1. A right of survivorship is associated with a:

   A. tenancy in common

   B. joint tenancy

   C. tenancy by entireties

   D. corporation

This question has two correct answers, B and C. Credit would be given for each correct answer (e.g., 1 point each). Unless points are subtracted for each incorrect response, students will mark all answers and receive a perfect score. Thus, the usual way of grading multiple-multiple choice questions is to subtract the number of incorrect marked responses from the number of correct marked answers. A correct answer not selected would not enter into the calculation of student scores.

The multiple-multiple choice type question can result in negative scores, although this rarely happens in practice. An advantage of this type question and grading system is that it tends to result in scores which accurately indicate the student level of knowledge. For example, suppose a student correctly chooses 18 of 20 responses in the multiple-multiple choice section of the examination. Suppose further that this student guesses on two more answers, missing one and getting one correct. The students score will be computed as follows: 19 correct - 1 incorrect = 18 correct, at one point each = 18 points. (Note that 18 is the score which the student would have earned if he/she had not guessed on any questions, and 18 is the student's real level of knowledge.) Thus, if students guess correctly 50% of the time, their score will reflect what they actually know. Obviously, if they guess correctly either more or less than 50% of the time, their score will not reflect their actual level of knowledge.

Many real estate licensing exams are composed entirely of standard one stem, four choice multiple choice questions with only one correct answer. Instructors teaching license preparation courses often prepare practice exams for their students, so it may be to their advantage to obtain detailed instructions from the appropriate testing service outlining how good multiple choice questions are prepared. All testing services have such "item writer" guides.

Matching Questions

Matching questions simply involve matching related terms listed in two adjacent columns. To illustrate:

1. Match the following methods through which land-use may be influenced with the appropriate public power justifying each method.

___ Taking private property for public use

___ Zoning

___ Building Codes

___ Subdivision Regulations

___ Extending utilities to a new subdivision at public expense

___ Title transferred to State when owner dies without a will and without relatives

___ Charges against real property used to pay for public utilities

A. Escheat

B. Eminent Domain

C. Police Power

D. Spending Power

E. Taxing Power

If the same number of choices is available in both columns, students may use the process of elimination to score higher than their real level of knowledge. This possibility is lessened somewhat by providing more terms from which to choose than are needed. Also, instructions should specify whether or not matching terms may be used more than once.

It is easier to prepare matching questions that recall information than it is to design questions that test the ability to apply substantive principles to practical problems.

Fill-in-the-Blank Questions

There are two basic variations of "fill in the blank" questions. Both involve sentences or paragraphs with words left out, and students are supposed to place the correct words in the blanks. The first variation provides a list of words from which students may choose; the second variation does not. The second variation is more difficult, because there is an unlimited choice of words which could be filled in the blanks. Fill-in-the-blank questions permitting unlimited choices of words are even more difficult when the subject sentences/paragraphs are open to multiple interpretations.

Fill-in-the-blank questions are used more frequently when testing children than when testing adults. Some topics, such as grammar, more readily lend themselves to fill-in-the-blank questions than do other subjects.

Listing Questions

"Listing" type questions simply request students to make a list of selected items under a certain topic; e.g., Please list the three types of co-ownership under which title to real estate may be held. Listing questions are effective when instructors want to test the ability to recall specific information. In contrast, they are not very effective in testing students' abilities to analyze and solve relevant problems.

Definitions

Requests for definitions of selected terms help determine whether or not students have an adequate grasp of important principles. An understanding of basic principles taught early in a course is critical to more advanced concepts presented later. This suggests that there is some sense to placing relatively more definitional questions on early exams, with application questions being emphasized later in the course.

Requiring students to regurgitate definitions in precisely the same language presented in class encourages memorization. But memorization is not a substitute for understanding. When grading definitions, it should be kept in mind that an understanding of basic concepts is the ultimate goal, and full credit should be given for different verbiage so long as all essential elements of a definition are included.

Mathematical Problems

Mathematicians sometimes state that "Math is truth." This simply suggests that some concepts can best be presented through mathematics. Using calculus to equate marginal revenue and marginal cost in economic theory is an example, as this mathematic procedure permits students to determine optimal (maximum profit) levels for business firms. This concept may be presented verbally, visually through the use of graphs, or mathematically.

At a more basic level, an understanding of mathematics is required to be a functioning member of society. Real estate agents must be able to calculate mortgage payments, property taxes, and commissions earned. Bankers must be able to calculate interest payments and loan amortization schedules. Chemists must be able to calculate weights and measures of various chemical substances. Each of these persons has to learn how to work math problems critical to success in their respective professions.

Obviously, placing math problems on exams helps teachers determine whether or not students have attained an adequate level of mathematical proficiency. When grading math problems, it is best to require students to show each successive step in their solution. Setting out each step enables instructors to determine student understanding of the mathematical concepts and processes, and to give partial credit for those steps worked correctly. This suggests that examination keys should be constructed to provide appropriate amounts of credit for each essential step.

Many adults have used math infrequently since completing their formal schooling. Thus, a major hurdle in teaching math to adults is to build up their confidence and to help them to realize that math really is not difficult. This may require breaking large problems down into smaller components and, where possible, presenting visual representations of the problems they are solving. For example, if the problem is to compute the square footage in a T-shaped building, it may help to draw a picture of the building. The building can then be divided into squares and rectangles with readily determinable measurements. The area of each square or rectangle can then be computed by multiplying length times width, and the areas summed to compute the number of square feet in the structure.

If the problem to be worked can be solved with simple algebra, it may be helpful to first set it up with words in equation form. For example, if a builder constructed a home at a cost of $65,000, and wants to make a 18% profit, at what price must the house be offered for sale? One solution, beginning with an equation in words, would be as follows:

Sales Price = Cost + Profit

Sales Price = Cost + 18% of Cost

Sales Price = $65,000 + .18($65,000)

Sales Price = $65,000 + $11,700

Sales Price = $76,700

Teaching students to conceptualize the problem is the key to building their confidence and helping them realize that they can work math problems. Math skills become rusty through disuse, but seldom does the failure to use math on a regular basis result in the complete loss of math skills.

Short Answer/Essay Questions

Short answer/essay questions typically are constructed to test understanding of how important principles have practical applications in the "real world".

Memorization is less useful than understanding if students are to score well on short answer and/or essay questions. The ability to analyze and solve important problems may be best tested by essay (and perhaps mathematical) questions. As used here, short answer questions are simply short essay questions.

Occasionally, students are heard to say that they score well on essay questions because they are good at "B.S.'ing." This is seldom true in practice, because most instructors have specific answers in mind for each essay question. Moreover, numerical credit should be assigned to each significant part of the answers being sought, with greater numerical credit being given to the more important parts. Assigning specific numerical weights to each important part also helps instructors achieve consistency in grading essay (and math) problems.

On the other hand, by their very nature essay questions tend to be graded subjectively, so interpretation of answers is sometimes difficult. Clearly, students' abilities to express themselves in writing can affect scores on essay questions. Moreover, some students may have the knowledge but receive little or no credit on essay questions because of poor communication skills.

Another consideration on short answer/essay questions is whether or not student performance should be marked down for spelling and grammar errors. Most real estate instructors do not grade either spelling or grammar on essay answers. On the other hand, English teachers sometimes make the basic point that students are unlikely to improve their spelling and grammar unless all instructors in all fields encourage students to improve. Whether or not spelling and grammar are graded may well depend on the basic purpose that a particular topic is being taught. A logical middle ground is to correct spelling and grammar on exams, but not deduct points for such errors. In contrast, spelling and grammar may be graded on term papers, because here students have more time to think about the manner in which they are presenting learned concepts.

Who Should Grade Examinations?

Purely objective questions, such as true-false, multiple choice and matching, can be graded by anyone without affecting the accuracy of the grading process. On the other hand, judgments must be made about how well students have performed on essay and other subjective questions. As a general rule, instructors are present throughout all class presentations and know specifically what was covered in class. Thus, scoring of subjective questions may be more accurate and equitable when instructors do the grading. To ensure impartiality in grading subjective questions, students may be asked to place identifying numbers on their exams rather than their names.

Additionally, when instructors score exams they get a better "feel" for the areas with which students are having difficulty. This permits instructors to do a better job of teaching when going over scored exams with the class, as well as determining which topics need to be reviewed further.

It is sometimes said that instructors will devote roughly the same total time in preparing and grading examinations, regardless of the types of questions asked. This is probably true. Objective questions take substantial amounts of time to prepare, but can be scored relatively quickly. In contrast, subjective questions require relatively less time to prepare but substantially more time to grade.

Evaluating Questions

Fairly sophisticated statistical techniques are available to analyze whether or not specific questions do a good job of discriminating among levels of knowledge. This analytical process is particularly important when instructors anticipate using the same question(s) several times with different students and classes. Questions which all students answer correctly and questions which all students answer incorrectly arguably are bad questions, because both are ineffective in discriminating among levels of knowledge.

Likewise, questions can be analyzed from the standpoint of whether they were missed by high-scoring or low-scoring students. To illustrate, assume all students who scored above 85% on an exam missed a certain question, and all students who scored below 75% on the same exam answered the question correctly. This relative performance suggests that the question being analyzed may have been poorly worded, or perhaps was even a trick question. Questions such as this should not be used again. Moreover, instructors should identify why the question was a poor one and use this information to avoid developing similarly poor questions in the future.

Particularly when questions are to be re-used, it is important to determine their relative difficulty. A four-step process for determining the relative difficulty of multiple choice questions is as follows:

PREPARING EXAMS AND EXAMINATION QUESTIONS

1. First, order the graded tests according to their scores.

2. Next, identify the top 25 percent and the bottom 25 percent of such tests. (Note: The procedure described next could be applied to all tests, but using only a portion of the exams is quicker and statistically reliable.)

3. For a given question, count the number of times each choice (A, B, C, or D) was chosen, and record these numbers for both the low- and high-scoring groups.

4. You can now compute a measure of item difficulty using the following formula:

Index of Difficulty = $\dfrac{\text{\# choosing correct choice in both groups}}{\text{Total number of students in both groups}}$ x 100

The index of difficulty is expressed as a percentage, and theoretically may range from zero to 100 percent. Since it is computed on the basis of the number of students answering the questions correctly, lower numbers indicate more difficult questions.

One additional step is required to compute a second index. Called the index of discrimination, this index is used to measure whether or not a given question does a good job of discriminating between the best and poorest performing groups. It is calculated using the number of correct responses in each group, according to the following formula:

Index of discrimin. = # correct in high group - # correct in low group
                      Total number of students in either group

The index of discrimination may range from a +1.0 to a -1.0. A negative number indicates that the lower scoring group of students performed better on a given question than did the highest scoring group of students. Therefore, larger positive indices of discrimination suggest that a question is doing a relatively better job of discriminating among knowledge levels.

When both the index of difficulty and the index of discrimination are computed for each question, rational decisions can be made about whether or not specific questions should be retained or dropped from the test bank.

An illustration of the calculation of these indices for a specific question follows:

Which of the following types of mortgage loans is most likely to contain a partial release clause?

	# Correct High Group	# Correct Low Group
A. package	7	12
B. blanket	27	16
C. participation	0	2
D. construction	2	6
Total	36	36

Index of Difficulty = $\dfrac{27 + 16}{36 + 36} \times 100 = \dfrac{43}{72} \times 100 = 59.7\%$

Index of Discrimination = $\dfrac{27 - 16}{36} = \dfrac{11}{36} = +.306$

Should Graded Examinations be Given to Students?

Some instructors never permit students to keep old examinations, apparently on the theory that they can then use an examination time after time. In this way instructors can minimize the amount of time required to prepare examinations. Whether the practice of retaining completed examinations makes sense may be determined in part by the nature of the students being taught.

For example, at the college level many stories abound about organized student groups with fairly complete files of old tests given by specific instructors. These old tests were not necessarily stolen, but rather each member of the group enrolled in a class may have memorized a certain series of questions (e.g. the first five questions, the second five questions, and so forth). Over time, organized groups can fairly accurately reconstruct tests, thereby giving future members of their group a competitive advantage over nongroup members.

Teachers faced with this problem may permit students to keep old exams, and even place copies of old exams on file in the campus library so that old tests are equally available to all. Moreover, handing back scored exams and making them available through the library may result in old exams becoming a learning resource. Instructors who routinely hand back exams and put old tests in the library argue that it does not matter whether students learn from textbooks, classroom presentations, or old exams. The important point is that students are learning, regardless of the source. Opponents of this practice, on the other hand, argue that recognizing old questions and remembering the answer does not always mean that learning has occurred. The latter argument also may be made when one group has exclusive possession of old test questions.

Another approach to this general problem is to require students to hand in their answer sheets but permit them to keep the question sheets. Students can then be given the correct answers supplemented by written explanations. This procedure may provide immediate reinforcement of learning.

Instructors and testing organizations attempt to protect their bank of test questions by never permitting students to see scored examinations. Students are told their score on the exam, but they do not know for sure what they missed. This makes it impossible to use completed examinations as a learning device. At the same time, guidance to students regarding their strong and weak areas may be provided by disclosing both an individual student's score and the average classroom score in each general subject matter area tested. By following this procedure, testing organizations maintain the integrity of questions with proven reliability in discriminating among knowledge levels while avoiding the significant expense of developing new questions.

Summary

Preparing good exams and examination questions is one of the most difficult tasks faced by teachers. Exams should fairly cover the material that has been presented. Ideally, tests should be graded and returned quickly so that they can by utilized as effective teaching tools.

Examination questions should be designed to test the level of student knowledge rather than the instructor's ability to trick students. The nature of the subject being taught often dictates whether or not specific questions should test the ability to simply recall or the ability to analyze important problems and find acceptable solutions to them. In this way, the alternative goals of recall or analysis influence instructors' choices of types of questions to employ, ranging from true-false to essay, and from objective to subjective.

Exercises for Chapter Twelve

1. List the different types of test questions available, indicating the advantages and disadvantages of each type.

2. What should instructors do when they discover "bad questions" on examinations?

3. What are the rules of thumb for determining the appropriate length of examinations?

4. Who should prepare examinations (i.e., instructors or their assistants)?

5. What are the advantages and disadvantages of (noninstructor) assistants grading exam questions?

6. What are the advantages and disadvantages of instructors grading exam questions?

7. Develop an acceptable procedure for evaluating the effectiveness of test questions in discriminating among levels of student knowledge.

8. For your next examination, calculate both the index of difficulty and the index of discrimination for all multiple choice questions. Interpret what this means for each question. Finally, try to determine *why* each poorly performing question did not do a good job of accurately discriminating among knowledge levels.

APPENDIX A

Generally Accepted Principles Of Education

Adopted by the REEA Board of Directors, 1990
Revised 1994

Category: KNOWLEDGE

Instructors should:
1. provide current information.
2. present alternative view points on material when there is not a single position that is accepted industry-wide.
3. clearly identify opinions as the instructor's opinion.
4. build a proper foundation for each major element of a subject.
5. deal with all key elements of a subject.
6. cover the material adequately in the allotted time.
7. answer all questions logically and concisely.
8. be informed enough to handle a variety of questions on the subject being taught.
9. admit when he/she does not know the answer to a question and volunteer to obtain that information.
10. focus on students gaining knowledge, not on impressing the students with instructor's knowledge.

Category: ANDRAGOGY

Instructors should:
1. present new ideas by relating them to pre-existing knowledge held by the learners.
2. teach at the learner's level.
3. show in a specific way how new material will benefit learners.

4. encourage questions and motivate involvement.
5. show tolerance - both to ignorance and disagreement thus avoiding arguments and confrontation.
6. build learner's self-esteem.
7. call learners by name.
8. involve learners in the learning process through planned activities.
9. use a variety of teaching methods.
10. teach to all participants, not just to those who show interest.
11. present key points by using examples as illustrations.

Category: SPEECH

Instructors should:
1. use concise, simple, and normal speech patterns, use simple terminology.
2. not read to the class.
3. keep the presentation on pace thus finishing the material in the allotted time.
4. keep topic flowing.
5. speak loudly enough to be heard by all.
6. enunciate clearly without being over done.
7. restate an individual learner's question to the group as a whole prior to attempting to answer the question.
8. use humor when appropriate to make a point.

Category: TEACHING AIDS

Instructors should:
1. make sure materials are legible, correctly spelled, properly numbered and mechanically produced using readable typeface.
2. use visual imagery when possible to enhance written words.

3. use written words when possible to enhance oral speech. NOTE: Written is better than oral; visual is better than written.
4. follow the prepared outline.
5. make sure that all material on the outline will be covered in the class and none of it is extraneous.
6. deviate from prepared material only to meet specific needs.
7. arrange the classroom so that learners do not have to look through physical objects.
8. use modern presentation equipment such as overhead projector or computer projection.
9. use equipment that enables the instructor to remain looking at the learners rather than turning back to the class to write.
10. make sure that the physical stature of the instructor does not block the view of the learners toward the projected material.
11. make sure that the projector screen is easily visible to the group as a whole.
12. use color.
13. use large images for projected material.
14. turn the projected image off when not in use and on to recall attention to the material.
15. never block the image by walking between the projector and the screen with the projector on.

Category: LEARNING ENVIRONMENT

Instructors should:
1. be positive towards the subject matter.
2. refrain from ridiculing either the learners or others.
3. wear professional attire.
4. attend to personal grooming.
5. set up the room to accommodate the approximate number of learners expected to attend.
6. make sure empty seats are kept to a minimum.

7. make sure that a lectern or table at front of room is unobtrusive.
8. provide writing surfaces for learners.
9. make sure that learners have ample space between seats.
10. not stand behind physical objects for more than a short time period.
11. use gestures during the presentations.
12. use physical movement during the presentation to minimize the physical distance between the instructor and learners and try to involve all learners equally.

APPENDIX B

Promoting Adult Education Courses

Introduction

Providing quality courses for adult real estate students in a competitive industry is a goal pursued by both for-profit and not-for-profit schools. For-profit course providers typically include proprietary schools, some trade associations, and continuing education arms of some colleges and universities. Non-profit course providers embrace some trade associations, academic courses at colleges and universities, and real estate related businesses who offer courses for their employees/independent contractors or to their customers for public relations or other business purposes. In the simplest sense, because many adult real estate students are course-price sensitive, for-profit course providers step in and fill the void when non-profit schools are not fully meeting industry needs. The important point is that profit and non-profit schools may approach course promotion differently, so some readers may need to modify the material presented in this chapter.

Attendance is not mandatory for most adult education classes, although in some instances either employers or state law may require attendance. Since most adults are free to choose whether or not and which classes to attend, adult education instructors/course providers whose income is related to attendance have a significant incentive to promote/market their classes to prospective students. The best method of promoting adult classes may vary, depending in large part on the nature of target audiences (e.g., prelicense versus post-license).

Cost Effectiveness

Regardless of the promotional/marketing method employed, in the final analysis it must be cost effective. Simply stated, the dollars generated by marketing efforts should at least equal (and preferably exceed) the dollars spent on promotional activities. In order to determine whether or not a particular promotional activity is cost effective, instructors/proprietary school owners must be able to determine how students learned about and decided to enroll in particular classes. Typically, this information can be obtained from a few simple questions placed on either class registration or class evaluation forms. For example, the registration or evaluation forms might contain the following statement:

I learned about this class through (check the appropriate response):

_____ Poster on bulletin board

_____ Direct mail brochure

_____ Newspaper advertisement

_____ Radio advertisement

_____ Article in local newspaper

_____ Recommendation of a former student

_____ Home page on Internet

In this way, revenues may be estimated for each promotional activity and compared with their respective costs. Promotional activities that are not cost effective over the long-run should be discarded.

Promotional Activities Available

Adult education classes may be promoted in many ways. To illustrate, a class offered to adults seeking to learn first aid skills likely would be promoted differently than a class designed to prepare people to become licensed real estate agents. A general listing of available promotional activities would include word-of-mouth, posters, flyers and brochures, free publicity, direct mail advertising, media advertising, and perhaps even the Internet.

Word-of-Mouth

Word-of-mouth often is called the best advertising for both products and services. Although brochures and advertisements may be attractive and provide desired class information, potential students usually are more impressed by positive comments from former students. To paraphrase a popular television advertisement of a few years ago, "when former students talk, prospective students listen."

Stated differently, word gets around about instructors' classroom performances and abilities. Satisfied students are cost-free resources that are quite effective in recruiting future students. To fully take advantage of and encourage this free resource, some schools periodically publish and distribute newsletters to former students.

Posters, Flyers and Brochures

Posters are large sheets of cardboard or paper on which essential information about adult education classes is placed. Posters provide information about class subject matter, time, location, cost, and who should attend. They often are multi-colored to attract attention, and may be either professionally or personally prepared by instructors and/or course providers. Self-addressed, postage paid registration cards may be placed in a box or attached to the posters to make registration convenient. Posters are relatively inexpensive to prepare, and can be quite effective. The key to effectiveness of posters is placing them in locations where they are likely to be seen by prospective students.

If several posters are placed in various locations throughout a city or community, distributing them to appropriate locations can be a significant task. Since posters typically are too large to be mailed without risking damage, often they must be hand carried to their ultimate locations. Posters should be in place well before a class is scheduled to begin so that prospective students have time to make decisions on whether or not to attend, and how to fit the class(es) into their already busy schedules.

As envisioned in this book, flyers are simply mini-posters. They may be typed or hand lettered, and be multi-colored to attract attention. Typically flyers consist of a standard, 8 1/2 inch by 11 inch sheet of paper. Delivery may occur via mail to a key person in particular organizations/locations, accompanied by requests that these flyers be posted in readily visible places. In some instances, hand delivery of flyers may be required to ensure that they in fact are posted for prospective students to see.

Flyers generally are less expensive to prepare and deliver than posters. On the other hand, because of their smaller size, flyers may be less visible than posters.

Whereas posters and flyers contain all essential information on one page, brochures are multi-page, and often multi-colored, attractive documents. Their length permits more information about class content, the desirability and location of classroom facilities, qualifications and abilities of instructors, and other information to be included for consideration by prospective students. Often brochures contain testimonials from successful and well-known former students which may be impressive to those considering attendance.

Brochures often are professionally prepared, typeset, and fairly expensive to publish in quantity. The expense of preparing brochures may be prohibitive when relatively small classes are anticipated and the target audience is not well-defined. On the other hand, brochures may be quite cost effective for larger classes, and also when a single brochure announces the availability of a whole series of classes.

Just as some prospective investors will not read an entire prospectus prior to investing, many prospective students will not read a long brochure before deciding to enroll in classes. Thus, the most important information should be placed on or near the front of brochures. Also, brochures can contain inserts containing class scheduling and pricing information. Inserts can be changed more easily and less expensively than revising entire brochures. This procedure may also permit the printing of larger quantities of brochures at lower per-unit costs. Distribution of brochures may be similar to the procedure used for flyers, but also may occur by direct mail.

Free Publicity

Many newspapers, radio and television stations provide a list of upcoming events of interest to adult readers, listeners and viewers. Such lists may appear daily or weekly in the same spot in newspapers, or regularly in the same time slot on radio and television. These calendars of events usually contain only essential information about topics, times, locations and course registration.

Placing adult education classes on such event calendars often is free, requiring only a telephone call or a short letter and stamp. In some communities, the calendar of events method of distributing class information is fully available and quite effective. In other geographical areas, media publicity about adult educational courses is only available via advertising.

Obviously, substantial numbers of adult education classes are taught almost everyday in large cities, so the likelihood that a particular class for adults would be considered newsworthy is quite small. On the other hand, newspapers in small towns may see particular real estate adult education classes as being newsworthy, and may even publish a feature article on them. Clearly, free publicity, whether consisting of a feature article or inclusion in a calendar of upcoming events, is cost effective and should be sought whenever possible.

Direct Mail Advertising

Direct mail advertising involves mailing flyers or brochures to prospective students. Direct mail requires mailing lists of prospective students to be personally compiled or purchased. If target audiences are easily identifiable (e.g., a mandatory continuing education class for real estate agents), the acquisition of mailing lists may be relatively easy and inexpensive (e.g., the list may be purchased or made available by the state licensing agency), and may result in a successful and significant ratio of class registrants per mailing.

On the other hand, the preparation of mailing lists for less well-defined target audiences (e.g., real estate license preparation courses where students come from many different backgrounds) may be relatively expensive in terms of both time and money. Moreover, the more difficult it is to precisely define/identify target audiences, in general, the lower will be the response rate from direct mailing.

Direct mail advertising is a science within itself, and both monthly newsletters and consultants are readily available to assist with wording and designing promotional brochures for maximum effectiveness. Also, articles and books on effective direct mail advertising are available in local libraries and bookstores.

Media Advertising

Newspapers, radio and television advertising is expensive. However, media advertising may be cost effective when large classes are anticipated and either topics or instructors are well-known drawing cards. Because of the expense involved, media advertising should be pursued only after careful research. In general, radio advertising is more expensive than newspaper advertising, and advertising on television requires even larger cash outlays. Without careful research and use of media advertising, the often quoted statement "Advertising does not cost, it pays," may not hold true for adult education classes. Testing the impact of advertising on a small-scale is recommended prior to committing to a large-scale media promotional effort and budget.

Newspapers will argue that the "permanency of print" is an advantage to advertisers, because readers can retrieve a paper several days after publication to obtain class registration information. Moreover, newspapers will point out that more people will see large display ads than smaller classified ads. On the other hand, display ads are more costly, so it is essential that they result in higher registration response rates if display ads are to be cost effective. Some real estate proprietary schools with continuing class offerings pay less expensive rates by continuously running classified ads with bare bones information and a telephone number to call for more complete information.

Radio and television stations will argue that they reach larger audiences than newspapers, and that prospective students will hear and see advertisements that they might not see in newspapers. Moreover, their arguments go, some listeners and viewers may not be considering attending adult education courses, so hearing and seeing course advertisements may actually create interest in attending classes. Again, media advertising must be cost effective, so different advertising strategies may be optimal for different instructors and schools.

Cyberspace

The explosive growth and use of the Internet has been noticed by real estate course providers. There is substantial reason to believe that more course providers will make use of the Internet in the near future. Many will have a "home page" which contains information (e.g., topical content, time, place, etc.) about their course offering(s). The Internet already is being used in marketing courses through the use of bulletin boards and/or news groups. Registration may also be handled via the Internet, and many believe that entire classes may soon be taught on the Internet. For those who have not been exposed to the Internet the following short explanation is provided.

The Internet is a world wide web (WWW) of computers which are interconnected through servers. Servers include mainframe minicomputers and microcomputers, each of which has a host name.[1] Internet users utilize browser software to file requests with specific servers, and the servers then execute and/or process these requests.

Within each server are located pages dedicated to a single person or firm (and the number of these pages is increasing worldwide at a rate in excess of one million per month). Thus, in order to use the Internet for class-related purposes, a real estate school might first create a "home" page that would provide information to prospective students and would also allow the students to address specific questions or comments to administration or faculty.

Both instructors and students must have access to the (WWW) if it is to be used to facilitate instruction. Instructors also must be able to access both authoring tools and a server.

Those using the web to teach may use Hypertext Markup Language (HTML) to incorporate sound, video, and graphics into presentations. Items which instructors might put on their server include the course syllabus, old or sample examinations, reading lists, and lecture notes. Interactive class registration/other documents could be placed on the server to gain information about student backgrounds and goals.

From the standpoint of course providers, the Internet can be used both to market and deliver classes to students many miles (or even states) distant. As such, it has the potential to revolutionize the manner in which real estate education is delivered and taught.

Summary

For many real estate adult education classes, promotion and marketing is essential to maximize income and profits. Satisfied former students who encourage others to attend by relating their positive educational experiences significantly assist with future class enrollments. Moreover, testimonials from former students are a good marketing tool when used on posters, flyers and brochures. Depending on target audiences, for instructors and topics, direct mail and newspaper, radio, and television advertising may be helpful in promoting class enrollments, as is free publicity. The bottom line on promotional activities is cost effectiveness, so it is important for schools and instructors to at least periodically evaluate whether or not their various promotional efforts are profitable.

Exercises for Appendix B

1. List the various ways by which adult education courses may be promoted.

2. What is the single most effective method for promoting adult education courses? Is there a single best method?

3. By what criterion should promotional activities be judged?

4. Develop a sample one-page flyer that could be used to market each of your courses.

5. Think back to the time that you attended adult education courses. What attracted you to the courses which you attended? Could the same promotional methods which attracted you also work well for your course and locality?

End Note

[1] For example, the name of the server located at Wichita State University is www.twsu.edu

INDEX

Acronyms, 96
Advertising, 186, 187
Andragogy, 18, 25
Anxieties, relieving, 20
Audio aids, 110
   See Microphones

Blackboards, 113
Body language, 101, 102, 105
Breaking the ice, 8

Cartoons, 83, 98, 116
Case studies, 53
CD-ROM, 127, 131
Chunking, 85
Comfort zones, 25, 43, 52
Common classroom problems,
   handling, 61, 63
Constructive criticism. See
   Feedback
Copyright law, 88

Discussion, encouraging, 50, 59
Dress, 101

Electrical cords and outlets, 39
Evaluation sheets, 11, 14
Examination questions
   definitions, 165
   essay, 167
   fill-in, 164
   listing, 164
   matching, 163
   mathematical problems, 165
   multiple choice, 158
   true-false, 156
Examinations, 153
   as a learning resource, 173

evaluating questions, 170
grading, 169
length, 155
preparing, 153

Feedback, 10
Feltboards, 114
Field trips, 56
Flip charts, 115

Game playing, 54
Generally Accepted Principles
   of Education, 6, 177
Getting acquainted, 6

Handout materials, 40
Hooks, 83
Humor, 93

Index of difficulty, 171, 172
Index of discrimination, 172
Instruction, evaluation. See
   Evaluation sheets
Internet, 188

LCD panel, 121
Learning environment, 33, 34
Learning objectives, 81
Learning pyramids, 30, 31, 109
Learning rate, 27
Learning styles, 28, 84, 109
   auditory, 28, 86
   kinesthetic, 29
   tactual, 28
   visual, 28, 86, 129
Lecture, 49
Lesson plans, 80
Lighting, 34, 35

Mailing lists, 186
Master classroom, 127
Memory hooks, 96
Microphones, 110, 128
   cordless, 112
   lavaliere, 111
   stationary, 110
Movie projectors, 122

Name tags, 9
Newsprint Pads, 115
Note-taking, 33, 41

Outlines, 41, 75
   chronological, 75
   format, 77
   problem-solution, 77
   space-order, 76
   topical, 77
Overhead projectors, 116

Panel discussion, 56
Pedagogy, 17
Podium, 35, 112
Presentation levels, 9
Presentations
   beginning, 82
   end, 87
   middle, 84
Professionalism, 5
Promoting courses, 181
   brochures, 183
   cost-effectiveness, 182
   cyberspace, 188
   direct mail, 186
   flyers, 183
   free publicity, 185
   media advertising, 187
   posters, 183
   word-of-mouth, 183
Puns, 98

Real Estate Educators
   Association, 5, 25
Research, 25, 74
Rhymes, 97
Role playing, 52
Room capacity, 36
Room design/layout, 33, 37, 129
Room temperature, 39

Screens, 35, 113, 131
Simulation, 54
Slide projectors, 123, 128
Slide/tape combinations, 124
Student background
   and goals, 6, 80

Task group, 51
Teaching methods, 47
   case studies, 53
   discussion, 50
   field trips, 56
   game playing, 54
   lecture, 49
   panel discussion, 56
   role playing, 52
   simulation, 54
   task group, 51
   town hall, 51
Textbooks, 41, 73, 74
Townhall, 51
TQM, 1
Transparencies, 116

Video recorders/players, 121
Videotape, 121, 122
Visual aids, 113
   blackboards, 113
   feltboards, 114
   flipcharts, 115
   movie projectors, 122
   newsprint pads, 115
   overhead projectors, 116
   slide projectors, 123, 128

INDEX

    slide/tape combinations, 124
    video recorders/players, 121
    whiteboards, 114

Whiteboards, 114
World Wide Web, 188
Written materials, 40, 73

About the Author

Donald R. (Don) Levi comes from a family of abstracters, real estate brokers and appraisers in Southwest Missouri. Don holds law and doctorate of philosophy degrees, and taught at the University of Missouri and Texas A&M University before accepting the Clark Chair of Real Estate at Wichita State University (WSU). In that capacity he coordinates both the WSU undergraduate and graduate real estate programs, and also has served WSU as department chair, director of graduate studies, associate dean, and acting dean.

Don is a charter member of the Real Estate Educators Association (REEA), holds REEA's Distinguished Real Estate Instructor (DREI) professional designation, is a past president of REEA, and was named REEA educator of the year in 1989. He was a co-developer of REEA's Instructor Development Workshop (IDW) and, as an IDW senior instructor, has worked with real estate instructors in 20 states from coast to coast.

During his 30-year career as a real estate educator, Don has authored or co-authored some 14 books, 40 refereed (academic) journal articles, 59 miscellaneous articles and university publications, and three chapters in books. He has received teaching-related awards at each of the three universities at which he has worked.

All of us are smarter than any one of us.

Sharing pooled information, ideas and problem solutions with your peers is the major benefit of membership in the Real Estate Educators Association. That's why more than 1,100 professionals are members. That's why you should join.

You'll participate in idea exchange at REEA's Annual Conference and at the Chapter level close to home. You'll receive the information-packed **REEAction** newsletter and the annual **REEA Journal** and Membership Directory.

You'll learn about awards and recognition for educational excellence as well as REEA's Instructor Development Workshop designed to fine-tune teaching technique.

Join today and learn about DREI, the REEA designation recognizing outstanding classroom performance and dedication to the highest standards in real estate education.

REEA
Individual Membership Application • Return It Today!

Name _____ Title _____

Organization _____

Business Address _____ City/State/Zip _____

Home Address _____ City/State/Zip _____

Send REEA Mail to: ( ) Office   ( ) Home

Business Phone (_____) _____ Business Fax (_____) _____

☐ $80.00 (U.S.) Enclosed

Please Charge to: ☐ Visa   Account # _____
                    ☐ MasterCard   Exp. Date _____
                    Signature _____

Mail to:
Real Estate Educators Association
11 S. LaSalle Street, Suite 1400
Chicago, IL 60603-1210
TEL (312) 201-0101
FAX (312) 201-0214